THE POLITICS OF
EUROPEAN UNION
HEALTH POLICIES

STATE OF HEALTH SERIES

Edited by Chris Ham, Professor of Health Policy and Management at the University of Birmingham and Director of the Strategy Unit at the Department of Health.

Current and forthcoming titles

THE POLITICS OF
EUROPEAN UNION
HEALTH POLICIES

Scott L. Greer

 Open University Press

Open University Press
McGraw-Hill Education
McGraw-Hill House
Shoppenhangers Road
Maidenhead
Berkshire
England
SL6 2QL

email: enquiries@openup.co.uk
world wide web: www.openup.co.uk

and Two Penn Plaza, New York, NY 10121-2289, USA

First published 2009

A catalogue record of this book is available from the British Library

ISBN-13: 978-0-33-523624-4 (pb) 978-0-33-523623-7 (hb)
ISBN-10: 0335236243 (pb) 0335236235 (hb)

Library of Congress Cataloging-in-Publication Data
CIP data applied for

Typeset by RefineCatch Limited, Bungay, Suffolk
Printed in the UK by Bell and Bain Ltd, Glasgow

Fictitious names of companies, products, people, characters and/or data
that may be used herein (in case studies or in examples) are not intended to
represent any real individual, company, product or event.

The McGraw-Hill Companies

CONTENTS

SERIES EDITOR'S INTRODUCTION

Health services in many developed countries have come under critical scrutiny in recent years. In part this is because of increasing expenditure, much of it funded from public sources, and the pressure this has put on governments seeking to control public spending. Also important has been the perception that resources allocated to health services are not always deployed in an optimal fashion. Thus at a time when the scope for increasing expenditure is extremely limited, there is a need to search for ways of using existing budgets more efficiently. A further concern has been the desire to ensure access to health care of various groups on an equitable basis. In some countries this has been linked to a wish to enhance patient choice and to make service providers more responsive to patients as 'consumers'.

Underlying these specific concerns are a number of more fundamental developments which have a significant bearing on the performance of health services. Three are worth highlighting.

First, there are demographic changes, including the ageing population and the decline in the proportion of the population of working age. These changes will both increase the demand for health care and at the same time limit the ability of health services to respond to this demand.

Second, advances in medical science will give rise to new demands within the health services. These advances cover a range of possibilities, including innovations in surgery, drug therapy, screening and diagnosis. The pace of innovation quickened as the end of the twentieth century approached, with significant implications for the funding and provision of services.

Third, public expectations of health services are rising as those who use services demand higher standards of care. In part, this is stimulated by developments within the health service, including the availability of new technology. More fundamentally, it stems from the emergence of a more educated and informed population, in which people are accustomed to being treated as consumers rather than patients. Against this background, policy makers in a number of countries are reviewing the future of health services. Those countries which have traditionally relied on a market in health care are making greater use of regulation and planning. Equally, those countries which have traditionally relied on regulation and planning are moving towards a more competitive approach. In no country is there complete satisfaction with existing methods of financing and delivery, and everywhere there is a search for new policy instruments.

The aim of this series is to contribute to debate about the future of health services through an analysis of major issues in health policy. These issues have been chosen because they are both of current interest and of enduring importance. The series is intended to be accessible to students and informed lay readers as well as to specialists working in this field. The aim is to go beyond a textbook approach to health policy analysis and to encourage authors to move debate about their issues forward. In this sense, each book presents a summary of current research and thinking, and an exploration of future policy directions.

Professor Chris Ham
Professor of Health Policy and Management
University of Birmingham

PREFACE

A hotel bar, spring 2008. I was explaining some recent developments in EU law to a senior scholar, expert in the politics and policies of West European health care systems but not in EU law. As I talked through the developing role of competition law and public procurement requirements, and other disruptive developments in EU law, he stopped me. 'What I want to know is, what are people doing about this?'

This book tries to answer his question. What are the people and governments who care about health doing to influence the development of EU health law and policy?

I have presented parts of this text at the Political Studies Association Politics of Health Group at its 2008 conference, the European Health Forum Gastein, and the European Consortium for Political Research Fourth Pan-European conference of the standing group on EU politics. For support and comments, I would like to thank Rita Baeten, Kim Beazor, Jeni Bremner, Cesár Colino, Raquel Gallego, Chris Ham, Nicolas Jabko, Margitta Mätzke, Monika Steffen, Hans Stein, Alan Trench, the French, UK and German officials who read various earlier versions, and an anonymous referee. David Coen and Jeremy Richardson put me onto lobbying. I have been very lucky to come across four extraordinary research assistants whose help has been invaluable and who each taught me a great deal: François Briatte, Elize Massard da Fonseca, Simone Rauscher and David Rowland. Connie Rockman was endlessly helpful with organization. My colleagues at Michigan were supportive, interesting and fun as ever, while the University of Michigan libraries never cease to amaze me with their breadth and organization. Karen and David, Margitta, and the Jarmans put up with many visits. And finally, enormous gratitude to Holly, far beyond what I owe her for reading it and putting up with the process of writing it.

Funding for the research came first from the Nuffield Trust and the US National Science Foundation Program in Law and Social Science. Neither organization, nor anybody I thank, is responsible for any errors of fact or interpretation.

London
October 2008

1

HEALTH POLICY IN THE EUROPEAN UNION
From Secret Garden to Public Park

Health policy is a secret garden to which few are admitted. Every country has its distinctive health financing, provision, regulation, professional organization, government bureaucracy and politics. International comparative statistics, and even detailed studies, find it difficult to capture the nuances of either formal structures or the way systems work in practice. So much is an effective accident of history and must be memorized; even useful categories such as 'social insurance' or 'national health system' fail to shed light on the tricky role of mutual insurers in Spain's health service or risk equalization in the German health care system. This level of variation and technical complexity is no surprise. It emerges not just because health is complicated and filled with groups (doctors, nurses, insurers, managers, civil servants) who have very different understandings of issues. It is also because health systems have grown up in relative isolation, with ideas crossing borders (often in distended forms) but organizational structures determined at home, by domestic politics and institutional. The result was health as a secret garden: difficult to understand, with high barriers to entry, and a virtually unlimited set of political and institutional peculiarities in each health system.

  That introversion of health explains why the development of European Union (EU) health policies presents such a challenge to health policymakers. With the development of EU policies applicable to health, the secret garden has become more like a public park. Not only can a wide variety of people enter without knowing or caring about the rituals, but also they can do many different things. In the space once confined to professions, social insurers, hospital managers and health ministries, with occasional entries by prime ministers and treasuries, we now find a range of different organizations, each extending its own model and standard operating procedures to the issue of making, influencing and implementing EU health policy, and potentially damaging, or at least changing, the core values of health systems (Ferrera 2005).

And so EU health policymaking is currently made up of the various extensions of bureaucratic models developed in other fields and for other fields. The EU institutions do not develop specific policies or forms of governance for health; instead, they extend the mechanisms and legal forms that they use elsewhere. Law on state aid to private actors grew out of policies for airlines and steel mills but now might question subsidies to hospitals, patient mobility law draws on general ideas about commerce to oblige systems to fund patients who seek treatment in other countries, and rules on working time that make it difficult to staff hospitals are part of a broad model of labour law rather than a reflection of conditions in the health sector. Only because of the EU do health policymakers need pay attention to member state competition authorities, or economic ideas from telecommunications regulation, or accept 'mutual recognition' of professional qualifications despite misgivings about each others' professional education.

Member states' and stakeholders' responses to these assaults on the secret garden, paradoxically enough, break down its walls yet further. The reason is that when they are called upon to engage in EU health policy, lobbies hire EU experts, who usually stress the importance of their specialized EU knowledge, and governments call in their own EU experts and rely on methods of EU policymaking developed in other fields. Rather than developing specific forms of representation for health policy, they extend their established models for EU representation, which are born of the interaction of their existing styles of public administration with the exigencies of the EU. And health ministries do not reorganize to deal with the challenge of making EU policy; instead they fit it, however uncomfortably, into their existing structures.

As a result, health policymaking for the EU is less a product of design than of transplantation and translation (see the two key texts: Mossialos et al. 2009; Steffen 2005). Most member states' EU policymaking, like the EU policies themselves, are not born of health policymaking and health policy concerns. They are a set of transplants from different policy areas and bureaucracies, and the development of EU health policy arenas, within member states and in the EU itself, is a process of adoption and adaptation of their models by the different actors who were created for a different world and now find themselves engaged in EU health policy.

This is a far cry from the politics of the secret garden, and it is not clear whether it will value or reward the skills and networks of those who specialize in health policy, know the ins and outs of policy-making in their particular member state environment, and use the ideas and techniques of health policy analysis. The emerging 'EU health policy' will be a compromise between the constitutional politics of responsibility for health within different states, the standard operating procedures of health ministries, EU co-ordinating and policymaking units, and the EU institutions themselves.

What is at stake is not just the autonomy of health policymakers – the traditional leaders of health systems – to make policy for health and with health arguments and evidence. It is also the extent to which the developing and still largely unformed EU health policy regime will tilt the scales in favour of, or against, solidaristic and health-promoting policies (Greer 2008a). The rise of EU health policy, and its assault on the walls of the secret garden, is the most significant and wide-ranging challenge to the autonomy of health policymakers today; it raises the prospect of policy being made, or constrained, by people who know little, and perhaps care little, about health.

Preservation of the power to decide in health policy requires engaged, informed, and active health policy advocates. Different stakeholders in Europe have begun to engage with EU health policy. An EU health policy community is discernible, albeit small, and more groups such as member state medical associations and non-governmental organizations (NGOs) are making ventures to Brussels.

But maintaining the autonomy of health policy and promoting health across policies also requires, above all, engaged, informed and active member states and member state health ministries. Of all the institutions with power to shape the future scope and nature of EU health policy, the member states are the most powerful ones that are committed to the defence of their health systems and their standards of social citizenship. The European Union institutions, especially the European Court of Justice and the European Commission, are powerful and effectively created EU health policy without any demand for it. They have their own interests and agendas, and their support for Europe's health systems can often be more theoretical than real.

Governments are not the most obvious actors on the ground in Brussels; they can settle into the background, grey bureaucratic buildings behind the carnival of interest groups, regional governments and itinerant meeting participants.[1] But they matter more than the carnival. The many stakeholders of the health sectors of Europe, such as professional groups, social insurers and all manner of NGOs, are collectively impressive, but are also fragmented. More important, they are only lobbies: by definition, influential rather than powerful. Regional governments sometimes have great power and ambitions, but without effective strategies and good relations with member states, they are little more than lobbies. Paradoxically perhaps, the autonomy of regional governments to make their distinctive health policies for Scotland, Catalonia, Wales or Madrid depends on the willingness and ability of their member states to represent their interests, as much or more than on their own much-discussed ability to lobby in the EU.

And what they do now matters more than most times. The EU is at a critical juncture – a time of undefined politics when what is being debated is the nature of EU health policy itself. The problems, goals, legal goals, actors and policy instruments are all still unclear and can therefore be influenced. We do not yet know how well a given health system 'fits' with EU law because so much about EU law is still being determined. Astute activity now will pay off more than it will later, when more options are foreclosed. This book shows what the actors are doing and why. But before that, it is important to identify what we mean when we speak about the EU. The European Union, after all, might be new to health policy but it is hardly new.

IMAGES OF EUROPEAN UNION

The whole problem of EU health policy is that most of the policies enter from adjacent fields rather than health ministers or health agendas. EU ideas, actors and policy instruments all come from different policy areas, as diverse as telecommunications, employment policy and social security. What is taking place in health policy is the extension of broad EU and member state models to health. So it pays to start by asking what the EU does. The EU might be new to health policy, but it is well known to policymakers and scholars. It comes accompanied by stereotypes about what it does – ones that not only interfere with a correct policy response, but also make it much more difficult to understand than it need be.

Two of the most impressive, resilient and popular stereotypes are the ones that try to capture the European Union's effects on health. One is that the EU is a threat – a mechanism to expose health systems to financial and thereby run down its expensive, redistributive and solidaristic health systems. The other is that the EU is the reverse – a promoter of a desirable model of health policies, the opposite of the United States and its highly inegalitarian health care sector.

The EU as a free trade zone

Some start with the fact that the EU is basically a free trade zone. This produces a basic argument that we should expect a race to the bottom. The argument is simple and well rehearsed and is compatible with data showing that the wealthy and those who enjoy the fruits of European integration most ('participating in European society') are most likely to support the EU (Eurobarometer 2008; Fligstein 2008; Haller 2008; Sauger et al. 2007). Social rights cost money. That money has to come from taxes (or, if they are pursued through labour regulations, higher labour costs). This puts firms at a competitive disadvantage against their rivals in lower-cost places. Politicians, finding that the cost of social rights is strangling their economies and tax bases, will eventually abrogate those social rights. EU structural funds, for all their public profile, are far too minimal to defend them. Investors and companies, and wealthy citizens who can work anywhere they choose, will move to the places where they pay the least taxes. Health care, which costs money, will suffer.

A perfect illustration of this argument for a race to the bottom was a controversy in 2005 when Swedish workers in the town of Vaxholm protested against a construction site which was using a Latvian company that did not agree to Swedish collective bargaining arrangements. The Latvian Minister for Economics, Krisjanis Karins, offended many when he told the press during a visit to Sweden that the Swedish trade unions were fighting for artificially high wages. The first time I heard of this, it was in a 2005 interview with a Brussels lobbyist for the public sector, in the heat of arguments about the relationship between health and a proposed Services Directive. He was invoking it, as were many of his colleagues, in order to argue that the directive would create regulatory competition, punishing Sweden for high social standards and unionization and rewarding Latvia (or, prospectively, Bulgaria or Turkey) for weak and badly enforced labour and social standards. The competition from Eastern Europe will, in this reading, eliminate the ability of a Sweden or a France to sustain the taxes that pay for their excellent health care systems.

Worry not, or not too much. There are two reasons that the EU has not, apparently, produced this expected race to the bottom. One is that the structure of the EU itself builds in harmonization to prevent just that. A huge part of EU legislation is just such harmonization, intended to keep states from dropping beneath certain regulatory floors. A nice example of this is the Working Time Directive, which regulates maximum working hours, including in health care.

The other is that race to the bottom effects are nowhere near as pronounced as we might expect from the clarity and simplicity of the argument. Some of the world's most competitive economies are highly taxed Scandinavian ones. There is an enormous literature on the nature and extent of races to the bottom. Their key conclusion is that races to the bottom are contingent, might not happen and, if they do happen, need not happen in anything like the simple way this image suggests (Goodhart 1998; Oates 1999; Rom 2006; Simeon 2006). Some political systems are disinclined to lower social standards, even if that might enhance their overall welfare. If a country is under pressure from competition, with increased chances of unemployment or loss of income, then voters' minds might even turn to enhancing their social protection rather than weakening it (Iversen and Wren 1998). Some political systems with high social standards benefit from the level of health, education and social cohesion that come from high standards of social citizenship. The benefits that come with taxes can pay off economically by enabling high-skill businesses, risky start-ups and stable, well-trained workforces (Hansen 2006) and a good health system, with a healthy population, is an economic virtue in itself (Suhrcke et al. 2005).[2]

The EU as a social model

If the EU is not a free trade zone that undermines social rights, could it instead be a positive force, producing quantitative convergence upward and qualitative convergence on something desirable? For some, the European Union is the institutional support that enables something called a European social model to survive in a global economy and produce convergence on a more, rather than less, generous set of social rights (e.g. Giddens et al. 2006; for analysis, see Goetschy 2006; Jepsen and Serrano Pascual 2006).

The presidency of the Nice summit of EU heads of state named the European social model:

> characterised by ... systems that offer a high level of social protection, by the importance of social dialogue and by services of general interest covering activities vital for social cohesion, is

today based, beyond the diversity of the Member States' social systems, on a common core of values.
(Commission of the European Communities 2000: 13, 20–23)

In health, a 2006 resolution of the Health Council (2006/C146/01) decided that the common values are:

- Universality (access to good quality health care for every person living in the European Union)
- Equity (equal access to health care regardless of ethnicity, gender, age, social status and ability to pay)
- Solidarity (a property of the finance systems).

The Council statement also discussed the importance of reducing health inequalities as a goal, and outline operational principles of quality, safety, evidence-based and ethical care, patient involvement and rights of redress. What will achieve these goals?

But beyond these words, what can the EU do to promote a social model in health? In general, both EU social policy competencies (powers) and the bureaucracy that promotes them are weak (Kleinman 2002; Robert 2007). The EU does not have significant positive health policy competencies (especially if we exclude workplace health and safety law, where it is powerful and has articulated a distinctive model, from the scope of social citizenship rights). There has never been much appetite among member states for an EU social policy competency. We can gauge this by looking at the health competencies allocated to the EU in the treaties. That is quick and easy because there are next to none (Box 1.1).[3]

Convergence can take place, of course, without the EU promoting it (Holzinger and Knill 2005). Perhaps the EU institutions' discussion of a European social model feeds into broader patterns of convergence. Here the concept of a European social model flies in the face of a consensus in the welfare state literature. To put it simply, most of the cleavages between different kinds of welfare states, and health systems, run through the EU (Castles 2004; Clift 2007; Esping-Andersen 1990: 174; Ferrara 1996; Pierson 2007). Jens Alber (2006) went so far as to see if the European social model, as seen in Europe's really existing welfare states, might include the United States. His results show that the United States fits comfortably within the spectrum of social policy indicators found in the EU (Alber 2006).

As a result, the abstractness of discussions of the European social model should be no surprise. If anything but the most anodyne formulation includes the United States and expels a few EU member

Box 1.1: *Article 152 (ex Article 129)*

1. A high level of human health protection shall be ensured in the definition and implementation of all Community policies and activities.

   Community action, which shall complement national policies, shall be directed towards improving public health, preventing human illness and diseases, and obviating sources of danger to human health. Such action shall cover the fight against the major health scourges, by promoting research into their causes, their transmission and their prevention, as well as health information and education.

   The Community shall complement the Member States' action in reducing drugs-related health damage, including information and prevention.
2. The Community shall encourage cooperation between the Member States in the areas referred to in this Article and, if necessary, lend support to their action.

   Member States shall, in liaison with the Commission, co-ordinate among themselves their policies and programmes in the areas referred to in paragraph 1. The Commission may, in close contact with the Member States, take any useful initiative to promote such coordination.
3. The Community and the Member States shall foster cooperation with third countries and the competent international organisations in the sphere of public health.
4. The Council, acting in accordance with the procedure referred to in Article 251 and after consulting the Economic and Social Committee and the Committee of the Regions, shall contribute to the achievement of the objectives referred to in this Article through adopting:

   (a) measures setting high standards of quality and safety of organs and substances of human origin, blood and blood derivatives; these measures shall not prevent any Member State from maintaining or introducing more stringent protective measures;
   (b) by way of derogation from Article 37, measures in the veterinary and phytosanitary fields which have as their direct objective the protection of public health;

> (c) incentive measures designed to protect and improve human health, excluding any harmonization of the laws and regulations of the Member States.
> The Council, acting by a qualified majority on a proposal from the Commission, may also adopt recommendations for the purposes set out in this Article.
> 5. Community action in the field of public health shall fully respect the responsibilities of the Member States for the organisation and delivery of health services and medical care. In particular, measures referred to in paragraph 4(a) shall not affect national provisions on the donation or medical use of organs and blood.

states, then advocates of the European social model must either do violence to the facts or operate with only the most anodyne formulation. Amidst such diversity, convergence on any concrete single model would be costly. The political, social and economic costs of convergence on a single model with distinctive, meaningful and European characteristics would be enormous.

But perhaps the defence of the European social model is that it is a valuable ambition. In many countries (especially Spain in this book's sample), Europe in itself is a positive value. It marks out not only a desirable club but also a set of desirable objectives. So defining a European social model, and appealing to it, might work even if the concept is little better than a myth and moral ambition (Loriaux 1999). The question for health policy is whether the uses of the European social model in argument outweigh the legitimacy it gives to the EU institutions. In some countries, especially France, opponents of some EU policies have occasionally taken up the challenge and argue against the EU in the name of the European social model (Joignot 2008; Milner 2005). That is rare. Much more common is to use the European social model as not only an ideal but also as a justification for the EU institutions. But do the EU institutions bear the weight of advocates of a social model? Answering that question depends on looking at the EU institutions as they really operate.

UNDERSTANDING EU POLICYMAKING

It is possible to argue forever about the nature, usefulness and meaning of a European social model, but meanwhile there are real

European institutions going about their work. They have predictable ways of working, policy instruments and effects. We cannot only study their behaviour in health, but also draw on their behaviour in general. As Chapter 3 will show, they are often simply applying models from other policy areas to health, with variable attention to the specificities claimed for health policy.

The formal institutions of the EU are complicated and will be discussed in Chapter 2. But like most highly evolved creatures, the complexity of its anatomy does not mean that its behaviour is complicated. The overall pattern of EU policy usually fits under two headings. The European Union institutions lead the way, especially in health, without there being much or any demand for them to act. And what they do that matters most is regulate.

Spillover: political and social extensions of EU powers

Explaining the expansion of EU competencies into health amounts to telling an old story. Health is one of the last major sectors to see the development of an EU competency, and its story echoes that of many previous policy areas.

The starting fact about EU health policy in health as well as in areas such as higher education and social policy is that member states have always been sceptical of it, with no support at all for some of the flagship EU policies such as patient mobility. Instead, health care is a case of what 'neofunctionalists' in political science call 'spillover' between policy areas. There are two kinds of spillover, and confusing them creates problems. One is spillover caused by society: for example, large numbers of retirees from the UK living in Spain have forced Spain and the UK to think about better co-ordination of social security and health care for that population. People taking advantage of one EU policy, such as freedom of movement, force member states to integrate other policy areas, such as long-term care. If low-cost air travel means more young Europeans break their legs on the ski slopes of other countries, then social spillover would mean that there would be increasing pressure from them, their insurers and the hospitals treating them to integrate payment and social rights. This broad, society-driven understanding of neofunctionalism is quite common and often appears to be what authors mean when they nod at it. I call that 'social spillover'. But it is not the necessary emphasis of neofunctionalist theory; European society and policy areas need not integrate for European integration to happen.

Rather, spillover can happen through political activity, even when there is no demand in society. This second understanding of spillover is quite narrow and precise: it is caused by the activities of supranational political institutions. The father of neofunctionalism, Ernst Haas, seemed to make this argument. In 1958 Haas explained the pressure for European integration once supranational institutions have been created as a result of the activities of domestic interest groups. Some groups, failing to get their preferred policies at the domestic level, will push for transfer of powers to the supranational organization. The powers, as used, will then provoke demands for more or less power to be transferred to the supranational organization. Integration in a policy area starts with interest groups and an EU institution, but once there is a supranational policy it rapidly creates a supranational policy arena around it, with groups organizing on the new level (Haas 1958[2004]: xxxii–xxxiii). This is *political* spillover.

The key thing to remember is that political spillover can be very powerful.[4] The EU institutions can take the initiative, and member states or voters cannot stop them. Return to the strike in the Swedish town of Vaxholm. The blow against solidarity in that conflict came in Luxembourg at the Court, not at a building site in Sweden. The Swedish workers' action would be challenged in the European Court of Justice, which ruled in the 2007 *Laval* decision (2006/123 *Laval*) that Sweden could oblige the Latvian firm only to fulfil the minimal legal requirements of operation, and not the requirements of Sweden's collective bargaining system, which underpins much of its workers' rights. The problem, the Court ruled, was that obliging firms to comply with the decisions of Swedish collective bargaining made Sweden a less desirable site for investment by foreigners and therefore constituted an interference with trade. The problem in Vaxholm was not a simple race to the bottom; it was the activities of a Court that decides based on the internal market more than solidarity. That is politics, not free trade.

Health is a perfect case of European integration – negative, deregulating integration – driven by the EU institutions without democratic legitimacy or an obvious justification. It is driven by EU institutions and produces markets where there were none, in order to make systems compatible with the EU internal market. That is why *political* neofunctional arguments explain the development of EU policy in health and social policy (Greer 2006b; see also the important work by Leibfried and Pierson 1995; Pierson and Leibfried 1995). The member states and others must react to the political moves of EU institutions and to the unexpected consequences of legislation they approved. They must develop the capacity and habit of complying with EU policies in health. And they usually also develop a specific health policy capability on the EU level, thereby legitimizing EU health policy further.

Political spillover, by creating and encouraging European integration, can create social spillover. Eventually there will be enough transborder health care providers, enough retirees in the Mediterranean, and enough Europeans engaged in health system arbitrage to create social spillover and integration, but that will be like the politics of EU health policy itself, a creation of the initial activity of the Court and Commission.

Once an EU political arena has started to develop, it creates a momentum of its own. On the most basic level, that of individual career strategies, those who have invested in EU skills and expertise – the ability to respond sensibly to discussions of esoteric issues such as the 'Altmark package' (also known as the 'Monti package') or the activities of an European Parliament 'rapporteur' – will often try to increase the importance of the EU. Often their jobs depend on demonstrating its importance to their superiors and seeking ways to influence it in their superiors' interests regardless of what treaties say. Many lobbyists spend a significant part of their time in this 'backwards lobbying', persuading their organizations to increase their resources by demonstrating the importance, potential threats and potential satisfactions of engagement with the EU. Even if their agenda is defensive, by arguing that their defensive work is important they raise the profile of the EU in health policy. And many lobbyists are in Brussels to seek some positive objective: better treatment for a given disease or group of patients. If they see an opportunity to use the EU to advance their interest, they will, and as a byproduct the EU gains a greater role in health care policy.

Political spillover was built into the design of EU and has been developed to a high art since then. The 'Community method' of legislation, led by the Commission, and the Court's development of EU law, have created EU powers where none were expected, created an EU political sphere beyond the dreams of most politicians in 1956, and have reshaped European society and politics. It could do this precisely because the supranational political institutions can take the initiative so often, in matters small and large, building new networks and creating new competencies. As they do this over time, they limit the options for policymakers and make unthinkable forms of Europeanization seem plausible.

And so the EU is coming closer and closer to doing all of the things that were laughed off the stage when a French health minister proposed them in 1953: common products and medicines standards, co-ordination of training and investment, shared resources and integrated research and training. In 1953 member state politicians could decide whether they wanted to integrate their health care systems, and they chose not to do so. Fifty years later, the individual decisions were prepared and presented to them by a supranational bureaucracy, many of them looked inevitable, and the global alternative of going it alone seemed irrelevant (Parsons 2003: 32, 86–88).

Governing the governors: regulation

By and large, EU policies that affect social rights are regulatory ones justified by the internal market – regulations on people who deliver services, such as professionals, and regulations on how governments structure their welfare states. They regulate the provision and finance of social services, obliging it to accord to a greater lesser extent with internal market and a few other areas of law. The EU, in health, does some quite direct regulation in blood (Clergeau 2005), pharmaceuticals (Hancher 2009) and medical devices (Altenstetter 2005). But its most potentially important policies, the ones that are truly breaking down the walls of the secret garden, are in the regulation of health systems.

With a derisory 2007 budget of 1.1 per cent of the continent's GDP, the EU has only one really serious policy tool: regulation, specifically regulations contributing to a single internal market. Creating the single internal market means eliminating barriers to movement and trade within the EU. Effective EU activity is usually about creating opportunities to challenge member state policies and vetting them for possible discriminatory effects (Wincott 2004: 94). The EU is a basically regulatory polity; it taxes little and delivers little, but constantly obliges others (including member states and regional governments) to fulfil ends determined in the EU policy process (Majone 1994, 1996; Mény 2001).

Regulation dominates EU policy instruments and the internal market dominates EU laws. EU politics therefore lacks the tradeoffs that elected politicians in the member states must make about social rights – tradeoffs between cost and quality, between timely access and universal access, between tax rates and health expenditures, between health budgets and education budgets, or between services for elderly people and services for young people. The European Union simply does not make those tradeoffs: most of the time what it does is eliminate them by systematically choosing freedom of movement and letting member states, societies and citizens bear or enjoy the mostly unintended consequences (Greer 2008c; Hassenteufel and Hennion-Moreau 2003). The EU calls the tune without paying the piper (Cram 1993). That is really all it can do, and its small grants and networking distract from that point more than they compensate for it.

Some of the most serious and persuasive scholars extend this to argue that the structure of the EU gives it a structural neoliberal tendency (Bartolini 2005; Ferrera 2005; Scharpf 1996; Streeck 1996). Their argument is that the EU institutions and community method produce deregulation through expansion of the internal market. The EU institutions are particularly good at removing member state laws and policies that inhibit the free movement of goods, services, capital and people. These barriers and policies, however, often turn out to have been props of some sort of social right; the UK's National Health Service makes universality and broad entitlements financially sustainable by using elective waiting lists to ration (Newdick 2009). By contrast, positive integration – the development of policies that preserve or expand social rights at the EU level – requires use of the elaborate, complex and unpredictable EU legislative route and is hampered by the treaties' weak social policy competencies (Schaefer and Streeck 2008).

The regulatory nature of the EU also means that it produces a strong 'ratchet effect'. It is easy to liberalize policies, deregulate and create markets; it is very hard to do the reverse. So, for example, the Republic of Ireland decided to create competition for its main social insurance fund (Voluntary Health Insurance – VHI) by inviting in other companies (Thomson and Mossialos 2007). The new entrants were quite predictably going to pick the best risks (the healthiest people) and destabilize the VHI. Awakening, the Irish government tried to impose a risk-pooling arrangement of the kind found across Europe, in which insurers with better risks would subsidize ones with worse risk profiles. That would not have been a problem except for the presence of the 'ratchet effect': imposing the risk pooling after the fact looked like discrimination to the UK insurer BUPA. It filed suit against the Commission, demanding that the Commission take action against the Irish government. The case illustrates how EU law can constrain policy options even more than it forces changes in current policy. Most of Europe's health systems could probably not be created nowadays because they would violate too much EU law. Will useful reforms in the future be made impossible for that reason?

METHODS

This study draws on a range of qualitative information. The most important data comprise interviews: 30 UK, 19 Germany, 23 Spain, France and 22 in the EU institutions – 9 Commission, otherwise lobbies and a Member of the European Parliament (MEP). These are officials, health service or finance managers, politicians (mostly former ministers) and political advisers (such as cabinet members or special advisers); the list excludes short conversations that did not include permission to quote and conversations with academic and legal experts outside government, Commission or lobby employment. The interviews were conducted in English or the interviewee's own language and transcribed for analysis. This is a very small and stratified sample, reflecting the organizational map of a small policy area; there is only one health counsellor in Brussels from each of these states, only six major repeat players among interest groups (Greer et al. 2008) and so forth. The diversity of interviewees and their small number is why it proved impossible to identify interviewees with any precision while maintaining their anonymity. The social nature of research in the EU meant that I was constantly meeting interviewees. I was able to repeatedly try out arguments in this book, and in return hear some information or have specific questions answered. They included attendance at seminars and events such as Gastein and presidency or European Health Management Association (EHMA) conferences, with the short conversations and presentations involved, repeated short interactions, especially with Commission officials, during which I was able to ask questions; and conversations or formal interviews with academic experts, many of whom are engaged in policymaking but who do not hold formal responsibility in the EU, an interest group or a member state. This was particularly useful for France, which also drew on François Briatte's interview-based research on France for Chapter 7. The book also uses 200 earlier interviews for other projects, including 30 interviews on French regions in the European Union conducted in Paris and Brussels in June–July 1997 and the interviews in Spain and the UK discussed in greater detail in Greer (2004, 2007b). They did not contain much directly relevant information, but certainly contributed to my ability to interpret the interviews here.

THE REST OF THE BOOK

This book charts the development of member state engagement with European Union policymaking. What knocked down the walls of the secret garden, who came in, and how? More prosaically, what has been the response of France, Germany, Spain and the United Kingdom to the challenges posed by the development of European Union health policies?

Chapter 2 describes the EU institutions' health policymaking. Chapter 3 charts the extension of EU competencies into health, both health services and public health. Chapter 3 reviews the most prominent ones. What are stakeholders and member states doing in response? In predictable neofunctionalist form, the political initiatives of the European Court of Justice and Commission have led to a response from a widening range of medical professions, health care organizations, policy advocates, private firms and academics. Chapter 4 discusses the problems of operating in the EU – challenges that come from its extreme complexity and that anybody who wishes to affect the EU must overcome. Chapter 5 then discusses the EU's developing world of health lobbies, focusing on their methods, and the systematic biases in who is lobbying the EU on health issues.

Chapter 6 draws on the extensive literature about public administration and member state adaptation to the EU in order to sketch the basic problems and range of member state engagement with EU health policymaking and then Chapters 7–10 show the responses to EU health policy in France, Germany, the United Kingdom and Spain.

Each of the four chapters identifies the member state's particular approach to EU affairs, including the formal structures, the way they work in practice, their engagement with stakeholders and policy debates, and their effects of the member state's engagement in the EU. Each country's officials, health ministries, economics and finance ministries, foreign ministries and central co-ordinators extended their existing models of EU policy to health. They have flaws, but administrative difficulty is often just a symptom of political difficulty, just as administrative centralization is a function of political centralization and hierarchy. The interaction between the political structures of the countries themselves and the logic of adaptation to EU politics explains how they behave in Brussels.

The Conclusion summarizes the argument. The secret garden of health policy in most member states bears little resemblance to the public park of EU health policy, and as a result both the stimulus provided by EU institutions and the responses of member states bears the marks of government organizations that have historically had little to do with health. Instead, their models of EU policymaking reflect many tensions, institutions and historic compromises within member states and the EU – of which their health policies and health policy interests are but one. Ultimately most dysfunction is functional from some other perspective. But that does not mean that there are no technical or political ways to reduce dysfunction. And it is worth seeking both technical and political solutions. Effective member states are the best way to ensure not only that there is a space for autonomous decision-making for health; it is also the best way to ensure that the odds are stacked in favour of health in European policymaking of the future.

NOTES

1   'Region' is standard European usage for mid-level governments including Scotland, Catalonia and Bavaria. It is an institutional form and has nothing to do with the presence or absence of national identity.
2   This is an argument that the EU itself has made: in October 2008 the 'quote of the month' on the website of the Health Commissioner is 'Health is Wealth', the slogan of the World Health Organization (WHO) Tallinn Charter promulgated in 2008 that promotes health as part of a good economy.
3   Although the revised treaty of Lisbon, in which an expanded Art. 152 becomes Art. 168, expands the competency of the EU to support health systems in, for example, cross-border patient mobility, this is not EU law at the time of writing.
4   It is hard to put it better than a UK citizen working for the Commission, cited by anthropologist Cris Shore:

> I suppose neofunctionalist theory is correct. Living and working in the EU does change you. I've certainly become more federalist in my outlook – not as much as some of those who have been here for ages – but I can see the process working on me. It's obvious really; you have a vested interest in promoting the EU because you live here and work for it, so your fortunes become tied up with the fate of the Union. You want it to become more important because you are a part of it.
>
> (Shore 2000: 152)

2

EU HEALTH POLICYMAKING

It is easy to both underestimate and overestimate the importance of formal institutions. Overestimating it is easy because most complex bureaucracies, such as member states and the EU institutions, have formal procedures and flow charts of decision-making that can fill pages and distract scholars; some accounts of EU policymaking have an air of unreality because they so obviously focus on formal structures rather than the (often much simpler) ways people work (Sauron and Lanceron 2008). But underestimating it is easy as well: sometimes the way it works on paper is the way it works in reality, sometimes the way it works on paper is a useful guide to the intentions of decision-makers, and above all formal institutions often underpin real power relations.

The institutions and policy process of the European Union are the stuff of much political science research (Bomberg and Stubb 2003; Cini 2003; Hix 2005; Richardson 2001). But an account from the health policy point of view is different, and necessary. One of the characteristics most important to understanding the EU is that it looks, and functions, differently in different policy areas (Mazey and Richardson 1995: 347). This account is of the politics of health, not the EU institutions overall.

TREATIES

In theory, the EU can do only what its treaties authorize it to do. If there is no power in the treaties for the EU to act in a given field, then it cannot do anything. By writing few or no EU health competencies (powers) into the treaties, member states thought they had guaranteed that the EU would have no scope to take decisions affecting their health systems (Stein 2003: 19).

The member states' determination to keep the EU role minimal in public health, and nonexistent in health services, shows through in the treaties they agreed. The bases for legal action in the field of health are poor, as seen in Article 152 of the consolidated treaties from which the EU gains its powers (Box 1.1, pp. 7–8). To a lawyer, this is a weak EU competency. The words 'complement' and 'encourage co-operation' are designed to emphasize that the EU may only supplement the work of member states, which are the main actors in health policy. That includes public health, where the treaty creates a competency that the EU can fill with legislation in the relatively circumscribed fields of blood and blood products regulation (a legacy of the 'mad cow' BSE scare of the 1990s) (Farrell 2005) and medical products regulation, as well as authority for agricultural and veterinary decisions to take public health into account (4 a–c). This article of the treaty paints an attractive image of the EU as a servant of member state public health concerns, with powers and policies only where member states have chosen to make it competent – in both senses of the word. The proposed Lisbon treaty created a more coherent and positive health competency, and showed what member states viewed as sensible, but it is clear that the EU would still be only a complement to member states (Box 2.1).

The treaty is also a profoundly misleading guide to EU competencies. Article 152 is almost the least important of the treaty bases affecting health care. As Chapter 3's review of policies will show, the problem is that treaty bases can create authority for policies far beyond what their original framers expected. Health is a classic case of this competency creep, with major relevant legislation being passed and major cases being decided on treaty bases that include no mention of health, such as internal market regulation, competition law, 'state aids', public procurement, professional mobility and social security.

The treaty base not only justifies EU activity by granting it a *competency*, but also decides the *measures* that it can use. The two key measures, forms of legislation, are regulations (which, once passed, are effectively member state law) and directives (which set out a goal and the outlines of policy but rely on member states to turn them into legislation and regulations that will work within their systems). Directives have more room for member states to adapt, whether by simply delaying their 'transposition' into member state law, as some routinely do (Falkner et al. 2007) or by modifying them.

Box 2.1: *Article 168* (*ex Article 152 TEC*)

1. A high level of human health protection shall be ensured in the definition and implementation of all Union policies and activities.

   Union action, which shall complement national policies, shall be directed towards improving public health, preventing physical and mental illness and diseases, and obviating sources of danger to physical and mental health. Such action shall cover the fight against the major health scourges, by promoting research into their causes, their transmission and their prevention, as well as health information and education, and monitoring, early warning of and combating serious cross-border threats to health.

   The Union shall complement the Member States' action in reducing drugs-related health damage, including information and prevention.

2. The Union shall encourage cooperation between the Member States in the areas referred to in this Article and, if necessary, lend support to their action. It shall in particular encourage cooperation between the Member States to improve the complementarity of their health services in cross-border areas.

   Member States shall, in liaison with the Commission, coordinate among themselves their policies and programmes in the areas referred to in paragraph 1. The Commission may, in close contact with the Member States, take any useful initiative to promote such coordination, in particular initiatives aiming at the establishment of guidelines and indicators, the organisation of exchange of best practice, and the preparation of the necessary elements for periodic monitoring and evaluation. The European Parliament shall be kept fully informed.

3. The Union and the Member States shall foster cooperation with third countries and the competent international organisations in the sphere of public health.

4. By way of derogation from Article 2(5) and Article 6(a) and in accordance with Article 4(2)(k) the European Parliament and the Council, acting in accordance with the ordinary legislative procedure and after consulting the Economic and Social Committee and the Committee of the Regions, shall

to the achievement of the objectives referred to in this Article through adopting in order to meet common safety concerns:

(a) measures setting high standards of quality and safety of organs and substances of human origin, blood and blood derivatives; these measures shall not prevent any Member State from maintaining or introducing more stringent protective measures;

(b) measures in the veterinary and phytosanitary fields which have as their direct objective the protection of public health;

(c) measures setting high standards of quality and safety for medicinal products and devices for medical use.

5. The European Parliament and the Council, acting in accordance with the ordinary legislative procedure and after consulting the Economic and Social Committee and the Committee of the Regions, may also adopt incentive measures designed to protect and improve human health and in particular to combat the major cross-border health scourges, measures concerning monitoring, early warning of and combating serious cross-border threats to health, and measures which have as their direct objective the protection of public health regarding tobacco and the abuse of alcohol, excluding any harmonisation of the laws and regulations of the Member States.

6. The Council, on a proposal from the Commission, may also adopt recommendations for the purposes set out in this Article.

7. Union action shall respect the responsibilities of the Member States for the definition of their health policy and for the organisation and delivery of health services and medical care. The responsibilities of the Member States shall include the management of health services and medical care and the allocation of the resources assigned to them. The measures referred to in paragraph 4(a) shall not affect national provisions on the donation or medical use of organs and blood.

If a member state transposes a directive into law in a way that does not command universal agreement, it can be sued by the Commission, which keeps a database of transposition, or by those who would have benefited from different transposition. Not only can a single directive produce different laws, but also it means that nobody should entirely trust a member state government that says a given policy is necessary to implement a directive. It might, but it might be overinterpretation or an unrelated measure the government is smuggling into law. Finally, the treaty base also decides the *decision-making rules* – unanimity or qualified majority voting for the member states, and the role of the European Parliament.

As a result, the importance of the legal basis, a seemingly obscure point, is tremendously important. It creates what Martin Rhodes called the 'treaty base game' (Rhodes 1995: 99). The politics of an issue, and the power relations, change with the treaty base, and so, for example, the Commission has proposed legislation under a treaty base that demands a majority vote rather than unanimity in order to avoid vetoes by individual member states (such as the UK). If a measure is deemed to be social security co-ordination, then it is probably a regulation and must be passed by unanimity, which means that it is tremendously powerful, but all 27 member states must agree to it. If it is internal market law, it requires only a qualified majority of member states, and the European Parliament matters. Article 152 creates very limited scope for EU legislation; if a measure is justified under Article 152, then it cannot touch the core of member state health policy.

COURT

Legislation is still relatively marginal in large areas of EU health policy, but lawsuits are central. Without the European Court of Justice (ECJ) and its willingness to follow its logic into health policy, there would be no EU health politics. The ECJ, 'the most effective supranational body in the history of the world' (Stone Sweet 2005: 108), is the high court of the European Union and generally accepted guardian of EU law, or 'master of the treaties' (Alter 1998). It, and those who use the legal code it has helped to create, are also the most striking protagonists of EU health policy. If the ECJ were more cautious, or did not exist, or did law differently, the field of EU health policy would be much less important, and much more in keeping with the desires of member states.

The Court's authority in the original treaties was originally quite limited: those who originally created the EU appear to have thought of it as a sort of referee in internal disputes and a check on the actions of the executive. Over time it has expanded its role (S. Schmidt 2008). To use its language, its decisions have 'direct effect' and 'supremacy'; they are law as soon as the Court makes them, and its decisions overrule those of member state courts. Furthermore, the 'preliminary reference' procedure means that judges in member states who think they have stumbled on an unclear issue of EU law may submit it to the ECJ for a decision. The ECJ, once deciding, tends to operate on what legal scholars call a 'teleological' reading of the treaties, in which it views the treaties as having an objective (*telos* is Greek for goal) of closer union and decides in ways that help Europe towards that objective. There is no particular evidence that member states ever intended such a goal, but the doctrine has proved durable.

Of course, the Court does not always opt for an extreme position. It is like any top court – highly political. It is clearly able to demarcate its competencies when it wants to avoid becoming embroiled in endless regulatory oversight (Stone Sweet 2004). Nor can we say it is insulated from politics; the best arguments here are the statistical ones that find it has, over many decisions, agreed with a majority of member states and the Commission, is indifferent to the preferences of the European Parliament, and rarely pays attention to isolated member states' policy choices. These relationships hold over many cases, which suggests firm structural underpinnings (Jupille 2004; Poiares Maduro 1998). Like most top courts, it does not normally make decisions that leave it politically exposed without support, and it has been known to retreat from such decisions when it does (Epp 1998; Obermaier 2008b). Even if its decisions seem to be ignored, they create a powerful weapon that contending lobbies and political forces might pick up later (Conant 2002; M. Smith 2005).

COMMISSION

The European Commission is the executive of the EU (see Joana and Smith 2002; Page 1997; Shore 2000, 2007; Spence 2006). It is a collegial body with a president, is appointed en bloc by the member states (each appoints one commissioner) and is subject to ratification (and a collective recall) by the European Parliament. The commissioners act collectively when they make decisions such as proposing legislation, but run their directorates with some freedom. Because each member state must have one commissioner,[1] there can be multiple commissioners per directorate general (DG) and some commissioners (as well as DGs) are in jobs that would not otherwise exist. DGs were once known by Roman numerals. Under Commission President Romano Prodi they changed to more accessible names, but immediately picked up nicknames. These were typically derived from the language of their commissioner at the time, and are often even less intelligible than the numbers. The DG responsible for health and consumer protection is called DG Sanco, a contraction of the French for health (santé) and consumers (consommateurs). DG Internal Market had a Dutch commissioner and got a Dutch nickname: DG Markt. DG V became DG Employment and Social Affairs and settled down as DG EMPL.

Legislative power, executive power and the power to network

The Commission enjoys legislative, executive and network power. Legislative power is simple to state: it nearly monopolizes legislative proposals in the EU (there is also a social dialogue process that has not been relevant in health). Giving the Commission a monopoly on new legislation was a masterstroke of the original creators of the EU. The institution most firmly identified with 'ever closer union' is also the one that writes the legislative agenda.

The Commission's executive powers are various, and limited mostly by the budget and imagination of the officials. They include funding interest groups and conferences, developing networks and scanning for opportunities to promote both use of existing EU policies and develop new ones (Cram 1997). The Commission, many defenders point out, is a small organization that employs fewer people than many local governments. This misses the point, as Edward C. Page points out (Page 1997, 2001). The Commission directly does almost nothing.

> The efficiency of the EU politico-administrative system derives to a significant degree from the fact that it externalizes the massive costs of governing the Union to member states. The EU is cheap and effective in part, because, of those involved in devising, drafting, and applying EU legislation, EU officials are probably only a minority.
>
> (Page 2001: 148–9)

From that point of view, the Commission is very well staffed. Few states enjoy a policy development machine with more than ten thousand employees. These thousands of people, spread across virtually every area of European life, account for much of the health policy activity we will see, as well as many of the points of access that member states and others use when trying to influence EU policy.

One of the things that the Commission does is sponsor forums, working groups and committees. These provide technical information, in the way that advisory or technical committees everywhere do. But they also increase the status, standing and importance of the EU. The basic idea is relatively simple. Governments, in Europe, compete for the loyalty of citizens and political elites (Greer and Mätzke 2009). The European Union, to win loyalty, engages policymakers and advocates by offering them opportunities to think through and promote their ideas on a European stage (Shore 2000). Engagement in a Commission forum on an interesting topic, such as the reduction of obesity, will not just promote good policymaking. It will also attract policy advocates who are more interested in substance than constitutions. It will start to make the EU into a normal, and perhaps attractive, part of health policymaking.

There are many kinds of forums in the EU, and even in DG Sanco there is an extensive apparatus of technical committees with delegated responsibilities in the consumer protection section. But in health, the networks are mostly informal and consultative and part of larger games of defining the nature of EU health policy. That is because it is legislation that constitutes more advanced committees, and there is very little legislation (Greer et al. 2008).[2]

The internal fragmentation of the Commission biases interest group politics: each DG tends to develop 'its' favourite lobbies, with industry cleaving to Markt and Enterprise, and health groups to Sanco. The chief executive of one major lobby even noted that 'We try to organize our connections through Sanco. It is important to put health into all policies, so we support Sanco'. That is a significant reversal of the usual role we attribute to lobbies.

In short, the European Commission has enough staff and networking power to make friends, build its contacts across the continent, and find opportunities for itself to play a role (and thereby build a European polity). It does not have the staff to inform itself about conditions or develop policy to anything like the standards normal for member state or regional governments; it depends on lobbyists for information and much of its thinking. And while it is famously open to lobbying, that means that biases in the world of EU lobbying such as are discussed in Chapter 5 can translate through to policy and legislative proposals.

Opportunism and internal co-ordination

The Commission has poor internal co-ordination, with a collegial structure that provides little political basis for directed co-ordination (Jordan and Schout 2006; Spence 2006) (one member state official suggested that I replace 'poor internal co-ordination' with 'down-right infighting'). At the same time, enlargement has multiplied commissioners and therefore portfolios (and therefore the number of EU level politicians seeking to make a mark). This makes the treaty base game much more complicated. The various DGs each have, more or less formally, jurisdiction over a given treaty base. The hier-archy among them, and to some extent their distinctive cultures, can be inferred from their treaty bases: for example, DG Trade and DG Competition are extremely powerful and autonomous because their treaty bases give the Commission impressive power and autonomy in those areas, DG Agriculture and DG FISH (Fisheries) are powerful but less autonomous because they are confined to clearly delineated policy areas where they are dominant, and DG Markt (internal mar-ket) is powerful but under constant political challenge because it 'occupies' the powerful and contentious rights to initiate legislation and enforcement actions for the huge body of internal market law that constitutes Europe's 'common market'.

Commissioners are not simply EU politicians; they are usually major figures in their member state's politics. They keep in touch with their member state governments and politics, directly and via the *cabinet* of advisers that each commissioner appoints. States appoint high-profile figures to the Commission in part because they want somebody who knows their politics well in a high-ranking post (this is also why they press to put 'their' commissioners in important jobs). The Commission (formally, the 'College of Commissioners') must agree a legislative proposal or lesser statement such as a Communi-cation that lays out its views. Individual commissioners, often repre-senting their native member states, can intervene to promote their state's position – in defiance of EU law, but perhaps as a good demo-cratic practice. According to two member state officials the powerful Spanish Commissioner for Economic and Monetary Affairs Joaquín Almunia held up and caused the 2008 Patient Mobility Directive to be partially rewritten in accord with Spanish preferences.

The nature of the Commission and the agenda of the President can shape legislative proposals and some enforcement actions, with some effect (such as a reduction in the power of DG Employment and Social Affairs and DG Environment under Commission President

José Manuel Barroso) but each DG is a strong unit in itself, and commissioners are not as strongly bound by collective responsibility as the theory suggests. We see the consequences under Barroso, whose priority was 'competitiveness'. On 2 February 2005 he told the European Parliament:

> Let me say this. It is as if I have three children: the economy, our social agenda, and the environment. Like any modern father, if one of my children is sick, I am ready to drop everything and focus on him until he is back to health. That is normal and responsible. But that does not mean I love the others any less.
> (Barroso 2005)

Focusing is not something that the Commission does well. The social agenda and the environment crept back in; Healthy Life Years became a Lisbon objective by the end of the year. We also see the decentralization in the failure of transversal policies such as environmental policy integration in the Commission or, even more so, health impact assessment. Barroso could not stop the Commission developing new environmental (or health) policy, but neither has any environment (or health) Commissioner been able to apply the policies to the rest of the Commission (Jordan and Schout 2006).

DG Sanco, the DG most focused on health, has two commissioners at the time of writing; one for Health (a Cypriot, Androulla Vassiliou) and one for Consumer Protection (a Bulgarian, Meglena Kuneva). The fact that it was split, that it is mostly still located in Luxembourg, and that both of its commissioners are from small recent accession states are all evidence that it is a weak DG.

Meanwhile, there are other, more powerful, DGs interested in health: DG Internal Market, DG Enterprise (focused on promoting pharmaceutical industry interests), DG Employment and Social Affairs (self-appointed guardian of the European social model), DG Competition (which enforces, and in some cases effectively determines, what is anti-competitive behaviour), DG Information Society (constantly promoting eHealth and the IT industry), DG Research, and, on the fringes, DG Agriculture (because of the close connection between animal and human diseases) and DG Trade (which negotiates world trade agreements that might reshape health law). All are more powerful than Sanco, all have distinct priorities, allies, treaty bases, budget lines and policy instruments, and none are natives of the secret garden of health policy.

LEGISLATION AND REPRESENTATION

Legislation is by no means the most important component of health policy in the European Union. In some areas, such as patient mobility, legislation is almost the last development. But it still matters and is what is most likely to stabilize the changing landscape of EU health policy.

EU political process changes with the issue because the treaty base determines the decision rules used. The study of EU decision rules is a small subfield of political science in its own right, but they are more intricate than they are complicated. There are two important aspects of any given legislative proposal. One is the voting rule between states, which basically means unanimity or qualified majority voting. Under unanimity, every state has a veto; this produces small amounts of legislation, very slowly. Under qualified majority voting, rules allow a coalition of states to decide over the opposition of others (the voting rules are very complex and include multiple hurdles, which makes it difficult to create a majority). The other issue that comes from the treaty base is the role of the European Parliament, which changes with the legislative procedure and ranges from effective irrelevance to an effective veto.

Put the different legislative processes together with the different kinds of legislation and the EU political process looks very different in different cases. It varies in the lead DG, the role of the Parliament, the voting rules for states and the possible instruments, and it varies by treaty base, which is loosely connected to the topic at hand. As Chapter 3 will show, social security law (regulations, determined by unanimity) is very different from internal market law (directives, determined by qualified majority vote).

European Parliament

The European Parliament is the directly elected representative body for Europe's electors, with 785 members directly elected from across the continent. Organized by pan-European party confederations, it has an amending but not initiating role in legislation (initiating is for the Commission, and final legislation is for the Council). It has played a role in some health-relevant legislation, such as the Services Directive, but it is hobbled by the fact that its legislation is not always the source of the policy and by the fact that under some decision processes it is not very important to the final outcome. It also has a problem fitting a *demos* (people) into its democratic function; there is very little evidence that Europeans view it as much more than an opportunity to register protests aimed at their member state governments (Bartolini 2005; Farrell and Scully 2007; Hix et al. 2007; Warleigh 2003).

That said, it is gaining in power, and in health the use of codecision on major legislation including the Services Directive and Patient Mobility Directive give it a major role. Essentially, the Commission produces a draft proposal. This goes to the Parliament, which sends it to a committee. The committee selects a member as rapporteur, and both other political parties and other committees can select 'shadow rapporteurs' who follow the issue. The rapporteur produces a report suggesting amendments, as do the shadow rapporteurs, and the committee then votes on the rapporteur's report (with the shadow rapporteurs' reports as the basis for most dissenting or alternative proposals). The Parliament then votes on the report as it comes out of committee, i.e. as a series of amendments. The Commission then produces a revision incorporating amendments it accepts. It goes to the Council. If all three agree (which is unlikely), the legislation can pass. Otherwise, the Council announces its position, the Commission modifies its position, and it goes to the Parliament. If Parliament and Council still do not agree, there are two more rounds between them. At the end, if they cannot agree, it fails.

European Council

The European Council is the meeting of the heads of state of the European Union. It operates in a way that suits member states: they set the agenda and what they decide in their communiqué is effectively passed, regardless of treaty bases. It was in this way that the first EU health programme, Europe Against Cancer, began; French President François Mitterand inserted it, and when the other heads of state agreed it, it became EU policy. For practical purposes, it operates by unanimity because its force comes from agreement among member states. It is the highest of high politics, and almost the only EU activity that appears in political biographies or memoirs of presidents and prime ministers.

Council of Ministers

The Council of Ministers is the effective legislative body for most EU policy (Fouilleux et al. 2004; Westlake and Galloway 2004). The Council is organized by sectors, so finance ministers have a council, agriculture ministers have a council, and so forth. Most of the time the decisions pertaining to health come from the Employment and Social Policy Council (EPSCO), which groups health and social affairs ministers. On this level, where the vast majority of EU legislation passes, decision-making is sectoral. Member states accordingly tend to focus their co-ordination on the Council. Most Council decisions are made ahead of time by COREPER, the Committee of Permanent Representatives – the member states' EU ambassadors, effectively, who prepare the agendas for councils and mark the issues as uncontentious or contentious. Most issues are uncontentious and pass councils without discussion because COREPER identified and sorted out differences that had made it that far.

Both the European Council and the Council of Ministers have a rotating presidency, with countries taking the lead for six months. The presidency-holder chairs all the meetings (and can call them when there is discretion), sets agendas and also acts as an honest broker. It must walk a fine line between promoting topics of interest (it is conventional to announce presidency priorities) and discrediting itself by advocating for itself. Presidencies vary substantially with the personalities as well as the capabilities of member states. It was common for my interviewees (from big states) to argue that smaller countries, such as Finland or Slovenia, were more likely to be manipulated by the Commission than bigger countries such as France, Germany or the UK. With 27 member states, the presidency is set to become a problem as member states lose their institutional memories of presidencies and more states with weak bureaucratic capabilities take on the rotating position. States with weak bureaucratic capabilities tend to rely heavily on the Commission and still sometimes fail. The failed constitution and Lisbon treaty would have eliminated the rotating presidency, replacing it with an elected figure.

The Council's formal process is relatively simple. After a Commission proposal comes to the Council, it divides into working parties in which the counsellors (subject specialists) go through the text based on their instructions from their capitals. Counsellors typically influence their member state positions, but by reporting their discussions with other member states rather than because they have been influenced by lobbyists (most lobbyists who lobby, rather than seek information from, a Permanent Representation are wasting their time). The working party eventually produces a map of agreement and differences, and the ambassadors to the EU meet in COREPER and produce their list of contentious and uncontentious points for their ministers. The ministers then meet and decide the Council's position.

The Council also works by consensus whenever possible (Heisenberg 2007). Voting rules matter, which is why member states fight hard over them (Spain and Poland fight especially hard for their significant overrepresentation). In practice, though, member states try to avoid isolating each other or casting negative votes. It is a perfect example of how informal process is backed up by formal rules. A good president will try to find a unanimous position. If that is not possible, he or she (the Permanent Representation counsellor in all but the highest profile cases) will go to the minority, point out the situation if the minority had not realized it, and ask if they could join the majority with small modifications to the less legally binding parts of the proposal (especially the introductory explanations, called recitals). If that does not create consensus, the chair will generally announce only the positive vote. If they have very rigid instructions or wish to make a political point, the losers can still announce their opposition or abstention.

ECOSOC and the Committee of the Regions

The EU, finally, has two high-level advisory institutions. One is the Economic and Social Committee, known as ECOSOC. This brings together representatives of unions and employers to comment on legislative proposals. The Committee of the Regions brings together leaders of 'subnational' governments to do the same thing. Neither is an effective forum or way to engage with EU politics and not one interviewee brought them up. The Committee of the Regions is slightly higher profile, presumably because it contains real elected politicians with their flair for visibility, because regionalism is more popular than corporatism, and because hopes for it, and their disappointment, were more recent (the 1990s).

REFORMS

There are many flaws in the European institutions, including Council voting rules that make it difficult to form majorities, the strange structure of Article 142, and the difficulty of operating institutions such as the Commission under old rules but with 27 (or more) member states. A consensus on the need for reform led member states to start a process of major change to the treaties. They started with a 'Treaty Establishing a European Constitution', which was a treaty written by member states on the basis of a draft written in an elite gathering under a former French President Valery Giscard d'Estaing. French and Dutch voters rejected it in 2005 referenda. Member states rewrote it, removing a few items and renaming it in order to avoid referenda, and it appeared likely to be ratified with most of its content intact until the voters of the Republic of Ireland, the only state holding a referendum, rejected it in June 2008. At the time of writing it seems likely that the Irish will vote again in late 2009.

Given that the Constitutional treaty and its Lisbon descendant were very complex, and that enlargement has not paralysed the unreformed EU institutions as expected (Dehousse et al. 2006), it is not clear to everybody what motivates treaty proponents. The pressure for a new treaty comes about because of dysfunctions in EU 'foreign policy', because there is no prospect of further enlargement in the Balkans without some institutional reform, because a Conservative UK government would probably resist any further constitutional reforms, and because of the sheer effort already invested by elites from across Europe. Moreover, the process of treaty-writing produced a document that captures most of the workable compromises: it is hard to develop anything better (Tsebelis and Prokosch 2007).

The absence of the revised treaty is a problem for the EU's functioning and for democracy. This is because the current Council voting rules make it very difficult to legislate. That might please voters who do not want the EU to act, but as Chapter 1 argued, legislation is only one way the EU expands its powers, and as Chapter 3 shows, it is hardly the most important one in health. The legislative process is where voters (via the European Parliament) and member states (via the Council) can best control the actions taken by courts and bureaucrats. If the legislative process is hobbled, that increases the autonomy of courts and bureaucrats (Tsebelis 2008). In other words, blocking the treaty on the grounds that it is undemocratic turns out to be a highly effective way of empowering the EU's least democratic actors – the Court and Commission. The problem is that the Republic of Ireland has no clear basis for a new referendum, and even the most pro-integration of the small states might have cause to worry if Ireland were to be ignored or excluded because it is small and inconvenient.

CONCLUSION

The formal institutions of the EU are complicated from a distance, but what is striking in interviews is how few aspects of them matter to any given participant at any given time. The legislative map might be tremendously complicated, but any given participant, whether member state counsellor, lobbyist or MEP knows his or her immediate environment and the ways to mobilize his or her institution effectively.

The most successful analyses of the EU focus on the complexity of its politics and the many opportunities to engage with it, if not necessarily influence it. If this chapter shows anything, it is that the EU is institutionally capable of creating major problems for individual groups and member states if they have not influenced its policies. If EU policy would create a problem for a member state, let alone a UK or Spanish regional health system, then it is up to that member state and its lobbyists to make the problem known, identify solutions, and promote them in the Brussels debate. The EU, like most political systems, listens only to those who address it properly. Health advocates and policymakers who wish to engage it must do so.

NOTES

1 A 2002 protocol to the treaty means that the number of Commissioners will be reduced and replaced with a rotation system in the Commission chosen in 2009. The Lisbon treaty would have reduced them to 18.
2 The networks build webs of connection but are not always fun or obviously useful, as 2008 interviews on DG Sanco's European Health Forum made clear: asked why the attendance is so much better than most EU forums, one top lobbyist explained that 'it's because they take attendance when [Director-General Robert] Madelin is there. After he leaves we all leave.' Another, speaking of the 'open' version of the same forum, said 'we all sit while the Commission talks, and then when we talk, they leave', later noting that the Commission's tight control of the agenda (specific questions posted on powerpoint slides) makes it 'like a children's class'. 'The whole thing is just so that they can say we legitimated it and we can say we were invited' finished a fourth.

3

EUROPEAN UNION HEALTH POLICIES
The Key Issues Facing States

With Simone Rauscher

It is necessary, but insufficient, to point out that the European Union is a regulatory polity that shapes health care systems by constraining policymakers' options and creating new forms of mobility for patients and providers. Nor is it sufficient to point out that the development of EU health policies, like the development of other EU policies as disparate as telecommunications regulation and professional sports regulation, is driven by political and social spillover. It is not sufficient to further point out that it is exceptionally difficult to stop processes of spillover; EU authority, if not an EU policy agenda, tends to extend over the whole of a policy area once it first starts to develop.

That is because the basic structure of the European Union does not tell us what kinds of regulation and what bodies of law will shape health policy. EU health policy is overwhelmingly based on the extension of 'adjacent' bodies of law into health, usually in the form of regulating health policymakers' decisions. Only a few policy proposals, such as those to do with limiting obesity or supporting health information, are of the sort that we normally associate with health policy, and they are the most minor in their likely impact.[1]

Which of these will be extended into health care, and how? Which of them will create the basic framework for governing health policy, how and how much will it be adapted, and how will conflicts between the different regulatory frameworks and member state laws and policies work out? Who will have what German courts call 'Kompetenz-Kompetenz', i.e. the competency to decide who has the competency? That is what is being decided now, in what political scientists call a 'critical juncture' and what we might otherwise call a crossroads (Greer 2008a; Krasner 1984; Pierson 2004: 44). It is easy to take a turn now, but in the future, a long way down the road, it will be costly and time-consuming and perhaps impossible to turn back and take a different route.

These policies might come from very different places in the EU itself, and appeal (if they do) to very different groups and interests within the member states, but they also come to a similar point in the member states. For all practical purposes, the list of EU policies could be equal to a month in the diary of the health ministry officials or lobbyists discussed in the next chapters. These issues are all known to them, and sometimes the same officials will attend all of the different events. The co-ordination and information problems, which we discuss in Chapter 4, come from the fact that having an issue be known to an official is nowhere near enough. It is understanding its impacts, understanding the politics, having the networks and reputation to act, and bringing weight to bear that matter.

REGULATION 1408/71

It is happenstance, but the traditional obscurity of EU health policy is captured by the obvious obscurity of the phrase '1408/71'. This is a shortened version of the number of the regulation governing the obligations of European social security systems, which include substantial health competencies, to each other and each other's citizens. It was inaugurated long ago, with the foundational regulation passed in 1971.

Because it is based on social security law, 1408/71 is rigid and under tight member state control. As a regulation, any legislation in this area passes directly into member state law, and so it must be written very carefully. As social security law, it must pass with unanimity and was usually the province of social security and labour ministries in the member states. The process was slow, technical and low salience, just like most social security law in the member states. Only in some member states – most of which joined after 1971 – is health decoupled from social security. They include the UK and Spain.

Regulation 1408/71 permits EU citizens to transfer benefits from one member state to another, or draw on benefits of a state in which they reside but whose citizenship they do not hold. That is mostly an issue of pensions and pension contributions that affects permanent migrants and retirees. But it underpins the oldest and best known (by design) form of European patient mobility policy. This is the old procedure of E111 and E112 forms, which are, crudely, about getting pre-authorization from the member state in which a European pays taxes for procedure at that member state's expense in another member state. This covers all non-emergency procedures; emergency procedures do not require pre-authorization under social security law. Further improvements in the co-ordination of social security systems are laid down in Regulation 883/2004 extending the scope of 1408/71. The forms have been replaced by the European Health Insurance Card (EHIC), which among other things is supposed to encourage use of this route instead of others, but the basic support for pre-authorization is clear and foundational. Social security law is conservative, requires that every member state agree, builds on 40 years of legal and policy experience, and gives member states the ability to control every last non-emergency case that they fund for treatment abroad. There is little in it to worry a policymaker.

PATIENT MOBILITY

Unfortunately for member states, health need not be only a question of social security co-ordination. It can also be a question of the internal market, or more specifically, the right to publicly funded cross-border health care services on the basis of Article 49.[2] This is the basis of the patient mobility cases that are at the centre of any discussion of EU health policy, and without which there would probably be no, or very different, debates about 'European Union health policies'.

The two foundational cases are *Kohll*[3] and *Decker*,[4] both of them residents of Luxembourg who procured services (eyeglasses and orthodontia) across borders and then submitted their receipts to the Luxembourg publicly regulated health care funds that reimburse them for health care. The funds refused because the services were purchased without pre-authorization outside the country. Kohll and Decker sued. The European Court of Justice ruled that the Luxembourg health insurance funds were violating the principle of non-discrimination by eliminating the rights of Luxembourg citizens to use services provided elsewhere.

This was not a legally interesting ruling in one sense: the right to provide services across borders might be far from complete in practice but it is a powerful one in European law and there never was an obvious legal reason to exclude health. So some law professors literally threw it away as dull.[5] In an area on the fringes of health care policy, abortion, the European Court of Justice went so far as to consider whether the Republic of Ireland's constitutional ban on abortion infringed on the right of English abortion clinics to supply their services across borders (Phelan 1992).[6] Orthodontia in the Low Countries is dull indeed, compared to Catholicism and abortion in Irish constitutional politics. But that only means that the Court was doing something top courts traditionally do when expanding their competencies: enunciate a major principle in a case with very minor practical effects. Policymakers, focused on the minor practical effects, do not fight the major principle as hard as they might. By the time cases with major effects arise, the law has already taken much of its shape.

That is exactly what happened with patient mobility. The twin judgments in *Vanbraekel*[7] and *Geraets-Smits and Peerbooms*[8] confirmed and extended the ambits of *Kohll* and *Decker*. In *Vanbraekel*, which concerned a Belgian national who sought reimbursement for orthopaedic knee surgery in France, the Court held that Article 49 EC applied to hospital care. This was confirmed in the Court's rulings in *Geraets-Smits and Peerbooms*, both Dutch nationals who sought reimbursement from their sickness funds for the cost of hospital treatment incurred in Germany and Austria. While member states may require prior authorization for hospital care, authorization may be refused only if the patient can obtain treatment within the state without undue delay. Confirming and refining the previous case law, in *Müller-Fauré and Van Riet*,[9] the Court refused to draw any difference between systems operating a refund system (as was the case in *Kohll* and *Decker*) and systems based on a benefits-in-kind scheme (as was the case in *Geraets-Smits and Peerbooms*). Moreover, the Court reduced the cases in which prior authorization may be refused by setting criteria for what constitutes undue delay, which was also at the heart of the *Watts* judgment,[10] in which the Court further defined the conditions under which treatment abroad must be authorized and made it clear that its patient mobility case law applied to all countries. In general, the patient mobility cases matter because they clearly establish the principle that the EU regulates health systems (Greer 2008c), but they might also contribute to patient mobility (for what we know, Legido-Quigley et al. (2008: 41–76) summarize the important Europe for Patients research programme).

SERVICES

> The Services Directive was an excellent example of people who
> hadn't thought through the problems suddenly rushing on the
> stage to say: this is the answer!
>
> (UK official)

> Even the UK and France were agreed. That means we can be
> sure it was a bad idea.
>
> (French official)

Once the ECJ began applying internal market law to patient mobility, it began to make sense to try to fit health care into the general
debates about services regulation in the European Union. The health
care issue fell into a major debate about general approaches, one that
basically came down to DG Markt, interpreting Article 49 with the
concept of 'services', and DG Employment and Social Affairs,
interpreting Articles 16 and 86 with the concept of 'services of general interest' (Box 3.1), with the constant possibility that DG Competition, or somebody else, would use the pro-competition Articles
starting with Article 81 to question the cartels, regional negotiations,
and fixed prices that underpin most EU health care systems.

**Box 3.1: Major treaty articles on services, services of general
interest, and competition:**

Article 16

Without prejudice to Articles 73, 86, and 87, and given the
place occupied by services of general economic interest in the
shared values fo the Union as well as their role in protecting
territorial cohesion, the Community and the Member States,
each within their respective powers and within the scope of
application of this Treaty, shall take care that such services
operate on the basis of principles and conditions which enable
them to fulfil their missions.

Article 39

1. Freedom of movement for workers shall be secured within
   the Community.
2. Such freedom of movement shall entail the abolition of any

---

discrimination on the basis of nationality between workers of Member States as regards employment, remuneration, conditions of work and employment . . .

Article 43

. . . restrictions on the freedom of establishment of nationals of a Member State in the territory of another Member State shall be prohibited . . .

Article 49

Within the framework of the provisions set out below, restrictions on freedom to provide services within the Community shall be prohibited in respect of nationals of Member States who are established in a State of the Community other than that of the person for whom the services are intended. . . .

Article 81

The following shall be prohibited as incompatible with the common market: all agreements between undertakings, decisions by associations of undertakings and concerted practices which may affect trade between Member States and which have as their object or effect the prevention, restriction or distortion of competition within the common market . . .

Article 86

. . . 2. Undertakings entrusted with the operation of services of general economic interest or having the character of a revenue-producing monopoly shall be subject to the rules contained in this Treaty, in particular to the rules on competition, so far as the application of such rules does not obstruct the performance, in law or in fact, of the particular tasks assigned to them. The development of trade must not be affected to such an extent as would be contrary to the interests of the Community . . .

Services in health came to mean a basic regulatory structure to ease cross-border competition in services of any sort around Europe by extending some basic principles. The two key ones were the 'country of origin' principle, in which providers are regulated by the state in which they are incorporated (so a French provider in Italy would be regulated by the French) and 'freedom of establishment', which prevents a member state discriminating in favour of its own citizens in laws governing their right to establish a business. Put together, this means that an Italian clinic dissatisfied with Italian regulation could incorporate in France (freedom of establishment) and then do business in Italy under French regulation (country of origin). Member states would have to make their regulatory processes transparent and not discriminate on grounds of national origin. The result would be, in theory, regulatory arbitrage in which the countries with the most advantageous regulatory structures would 'win' and other member states would face pressure to converge on their laws. The problems of asking the French regulators to guarantee the quality of a provider operating in Italy should be obvious.[11]

The alternative, 'services of general economic interest' (and the more nebulous 'services of general interest') arose because many policymakers disliked such prospects and also worried that cross-subsidies would be wiped out by the increased competition. The concept underlying it was that some services required a different regulatory framework – tighter with regards to some public duties such as universal access, and looser with regards to liberalizing measures that might promote so much competition as to damage solidarity and redistribution. It has a weaker legal basis and in recent years Employment and Social Affairs has been somewhat weaker than Markt: Markt offers the prospect of liberalization and competitiveness, while DG Employment and Social Affairs' guardianship of the European social model fell out of favour. It has been kept alive in good part by the French, who argued for years that health, like many areas of social policy and utilities, was a service of general interest and should be viewed as such.

Services of General Economic Interest was the first concept to appear in health, when a 2003 Green Paper (COM(2003)270) incorporated it.[12] This triggered extensive consultations on the issue and absorbed quite a lot of the energy of interest groups in Brussels. It came as a surprise for them and many others when health care services next appeared, incorporated into the legislative proposal for a general Services Directive (COM(2004)2) in Europe. The draft Services Directive was the fruit of a Commission conviction that much of Europe's low productivity and growth, compared to the United States, came from its over-regulated services sector. Over and over again, such an identification of a European problem is the entrée for a Commission proposal to solve it with the extension of a European market, and so it was in this case (Jabko 2006). The surprise was finding health care included. The Commission's consistent pretext was that the Services Directive merely codified what was already developing in the Court's decisions; in other words, the Court's logic led to Freedom of Establishment and Non-discrimination, and so it would only stabilize the legal situation to fold the health care sector into the Services Directive. Member states – apparently all the member states – and almost all of the health care lobbies in Brussels were unconvinced.

The Services Directive as a whole had a bad reception in Brussels and, under the name 'Bolkestein Directive' (after the abrasive Dutch Commissioner for DG Markt), became unpopular across much of the EU. The European Parliament finally passed it but without the country of origin principle and without health. There are still advocates for health as a service of general (economic) interest and there are still many groups, including some in DG Markt, who would be willing to continue applying services (Art. 49) law to health services where possible. In the short term, however, these two options demonstrated that health was going to get a specific legal structure of its own, something the EP requested at the conclusion of the Services Directive debates.

HEALTH LEGISLATION: THE PATIENT MOBILITY DIRECTIVE

That specific health law, the Patient Mobility Directive (COM(2008)-414), is now under consideration. It emerged from the confluence of three things: member states' demand for 'legal certainty' (and, implicitly, some control over a process driven by the ECJ), the failure of alternative frameworks such as the Services Directive or Services of General Interest (the latter in part because there was too much distinctive ECJ health jurisprudence) and the awakening of more EU health care sector actors to the issue, many of whom did not like what they saw.

The Directive was led by DG Sanco and based on a long consultation with many different stakeholders invited to submit opinions formally; the Commission official most responsible for drafting it also travelled to visit many stakeholders, both presenting its virtues (at least relative to ECJ decision-making) and seeking some feedback. It was supposed to come out in 2007, and deliberately leaked copies drifted around Brussels in at least four versions, but it was delayed in the College of Commissioners. It finally emerged, amended, in June 2008.

As proposed, the directive would allow patients to travel abroad freely for non-hospital care funded by their home systems, but allow pre-authorization requirements for hospitals (and, according to one Commission official, especially expensive outpatient treatment). It does not offer anything particularly attractive: there need be no help with travel or hotel costs; patients are reimbursed afterward, so they have to have cash; and they are reimbursed at the rates of their home member state rather than the one in which they seek treatment. The inequitable aspects of the directive make sense if we consider the incentive that member states (and many patients) have to operate through social security processes that allow pre-authorization, fully funded care, and some integration of care home and abroad in order to reduce the risks. Member states are to establish points of contact that collect and present useful information about quality and risks. This is a problem, given that most EU states have not tried to establish such registers; the ones that have, generally have failed; and there are very serious debates about what makes useful quality indicators at all. The logic of a single point of contact and transparency is one common in EU legislation, and combines apparent modesty with a major expansion of EU competencies, but in this case it is very difficult to imagine it being implemented. For health services experts not sufficiently astonished by these proposals, it also proposed a dispute settlement procedure that would have either trumped or harmonized medical malpractice law and suggested that systems would need to establish clear 'baskets' of covered services. Some have, but others, such as the UK, have not needed them because they used gatekeeping systems to determine what patients needed.

One of the most interesting features of the proposed legislation is that it completes a shift in the framing of policies. For years, the Court's decisions leaned heavily on the rights of providers: making Mrs Watts get her treatment in the UK discriminated in favour of the UK providers and against the French. This commercial framing probably did not help the cause of EU law, as the Services Directive debates showed. Important Brussels lobbies were already in February 2006 – just after the Services Directive's amended passage – framing patient safety as a crucial, 'umbrella' issue. So drafts of the legislation that leaked in 2007 became steadily more focused on the rights of patients, presenting the issue as one of patients' rights to enjoy health care benefits across Europe. At a conference in Bad

Hofgastein, Austria, in 2008, John Bowis MEP, a UK Conservative and the European Parliament rapporteur on the Patient Mobility Directive, commented on how he repeatedly told the Commission to ban the word 'services' and make it about patients in order to get it passed.

As of autumn 2008 the proposed directive was in the European Parliament. Bowis aspired to pass it on the first reading of codecision, but that is highly unlikely given disagreement among member states. So the proposed directive will probably remain in the legislative process into late 2009, or even 2010, because there are European Parliament elections in 2009, because many stakeholders and even states do not like the principle of patient mobility, and because (despite all the talk of patients), the main argument for the directive is not that it is especially good policy, but rather that it codifies and might slow ECJ decisions.

QUALITY AND SUPPORT FOR HEALTH SERVICES

Once the agenda is about patients, rather than services or the four freedoms, all sorts of initiatives can be reframed and presented as integral parts of the EU agenda. The EU, like any government, attracts advocates who are more interested in their policies than in the allocation of authority between different levels of government: 'men's health', for example, is a cause visible mostly at the EU level because its advocates are effective at raising funds and using them to gain visibility at the EU level. The most dramatic case of health advocates gaining support for an EU-level initiative is probably that of cancer, where the cancer network dating back to Mitterrand's intervention developed a powerful life of its own (Trubek et al. 2009). But advocates for EU involvement in specific aspects of care come into their own with the development of not only an EU health policy arena, but also health as a specific area of EU policy.

Simply put, a positive agenda fulfilling the focus on patients is necessary because the European Union has to offer something positive to health policymakers; imposing new regulatory constraints alone is a poor way to build support and constituencies. It can then draw on the advocates – the many people who do have a genuine commitment to improving health care and health outcomes, and often to specific ideas such as eHealth. Such policy advocates, if they want to be effective, do not enjoy the luxury of focusing on only one level of government. So if the EU is interested in developing a policy to support health care, there will be a guaranteed supply of policies from various policy advocates.

The policy ideas tend to hover around DG Sanco, which has the best relationships with European health policy communities.[13] They focus on ways that the EU institutions can support health care – most often by positive actions such as conferences rather than by the much more difficult (if potentially very rewarding) project of truly making health part of all EU policies. Small-scale contributions offer all sorts of possible alliances. The health strategy for 2008–2013 (COM(2008)630) is a collection of such ideas: objectives include 'citizens' empowerment', health literacy programmes, guidelines on cancer screening and 'measures to promote the health of older people and the workforce and actions on children's health'. The importance of children's health and cancer screening, rather than the value or legitimacy of EU involvement, is the basis of the argument.

A particularly clear example of policy advocates connecting with DGs to create EU programs is eHealth. Every presidency since 2004 has had a conference on eHealth – an interesting topic, one conducive to European integration (easing cross-border treatment), one that aids alliances within the Commission (with DG Information Society), one that engages powerful IT industry actors, and yet one that has limited EU competencies. Another is the inclusion of health as a suitable basis for receiving funding from the relatively large European Social Fund. The pull factor should lead to a large number of health actors becoming interested in the EU once they realize the money is available (for contributing to goals that appear to have been copied directly from the Open Method of Co-ordination's goals for health – a nice way for DG EMPL to strengthen that process).

Finally, beyond the attractions of work reducing cancer or winning European Social Funds grants, the interaction with the Patient Mobility Directive promises a bright future for such actions on health care. The next step after patient mobility, of course, is quality – a short step from both a focus on patients' rights and on measures that underpin good health systems. As far back as 2005, an interviewee (a UK EU specialist not working in health) asked me about patient mobility law; after I explained the basic issue, his immediate response was to say, 'That will create pressure for common standards from the Commission'. In 2008 Commission officials were careful to stress that all they sought was transparency (through the difficult-to-implement quality reporting standards in the proposed directive) and whatever quality improvements that might create, but others were clear that what they sought was EU quality standards.

WORKING TIME DIRECTIVE

The 1993 Working Time Directive 93/104/EC,[14] now replaced by Directive 2003/34/EC,[15] lays down provisions for a maximum 48-hour working week (including overtime), rest periods and breaks and a minimum of four weeks' paid leave per year, to protect workers from adverse health and safety risks. The Working Time Directive (WTD) only occasionally makes special provisions for health care professionals but, provided health care professionals satisfy the status of 'employee' or 'worker', treats them the same way workers in other industries are treated (Hervey and McHale 2004).

This approach has been criticized by health care professionals and providers of health care as being insufficiently sensitive to the traditional practices inherent in the health care systems of many member states. The resulting difficulties have led to several cases brought before the ECJ for clarification (Hervey and McHale 2004). Spanish legislation, for instance, provided for a 40-hour working week for staff in primary health care teams without prejudice to work that such staff were required to undertake while being on call. This provision was challenged in the *SiMAP* case,[16] on the grounds that working time should not exceed set limits as laid out in the WTD. The Court confirmed that the Working Time Directive also applies to workers in primary care teams and went on to find that the time professionals spend at the place of employment available for work during 'on-call' time falls within the scope of the WTD. In *Jaeger*,[17] a case involving a hospital doctor in Kiel, Germany, the Court went even further and ruled that the time on-call hospital doctors are present in the hospital and contactable counts as working time even when the doctor is actually asleep during some or all of this time (Hervey and McHale 2004).

The clarifications in *SiMAP* and *Jaeger* have had substantial impacts on hospital practices in the majority of member states. Implementing the Working Time Directive has proven difficult or almost impossible and currently only a handful of European countries – including Sweden, Denmark and the Netherlands – comply with the existing regulations (Pounder 2006). In Germany, for instance, hospitals would need to recruit roughly 27,000 new physicians to comply with the WTD.[18] There are, however, fewer than

4000 unemployed doctors in Germany, making it impossible for German hospitals to fill the gaps that the provisions of the WTD have created.[19] In Scotland, a manager in the National Health Service (NHS) explained to me in September 2008 that 'we all have appointed leads to implement the Directive, but nothing happens because nobody knows how we can possibly comply.'

Trainee doctors' hours are the most problematic. Restrictions of the long hours that have traditionally formed part of junior doctors' training have caused capacity problems and have resulted in the WTD being criticized as insufficiently sensitive to the traditional practices of European health care systems (Hervey and McHale 2004; Pounder 2006). Such criticisms led to an amendment of the WTD in 2000 in the form of Directive 2000/34/EC,[20] which allows member states to derogate from the WTD's provisions regarding the maximum weekly working time for junior doctors, for a transitional period of five years. As a result, in countries such as the UK, which opted out of the WTD, the maximum work hours for junior doctors have remained at 58 hours but were due to be reduced to 48 hours in 2009, representing a major challenge for organizing and financing the British health system.

The WTD has been on the brink of reform for years. Any reform would effectively reverse *Jaeger* and *SiMAP*. The problem, however, is that many member states, lobbies and MEPs would also like any reform to eliminate the UK's opt-out. In 2005 the UK presidency thought it had brokered a compromise, and in 2008 the UK made a deal that preserved its opt-out in return for giving way on separate legislation covering the rights of agency workers. In each case, the legislation would have allowed member states to undo the restriction to trainees' hours. In each case, the enormous ease with which member states can block legislation in the Council stopped changes without even testing the power in the European Parliament of groups that support the WTD in health as it stands or oppose the UK opt-out.

PROFESSIONAL MOBILITY

Professional mobility is influenced by EU law on the freedom of establishment as spelled out in Articles 34 to 48 of the treaty, but more importantly by so-called sectoral directives on the mutual recognition of qualifications in the context of the free movement of persons. Health professionals were the first professional group to be

the subject of secondary European legislation facilitating free movement and among health professionals, doctors were the first to receive
attention (Peeters et al. 2009). The mutual recognition of doctors'
qualifications was originally covered in Directive 75/362/EEC[21] and
Directive 75/363/EEC[22] (later codified in the Doctors' Directive 93/
16)[23] which have become the model for sectoral directives for other
health professions: nurses, dentists, veterinary surgeons, midwives
and pharmacists. The remaining categories of health professionals
fell under the scope of the general directives (Peeters et al. 2009;
Zimmermann 2008).

Directive 2005/36/EC[24] consolidates and modernizes the rules regulating the recognition of professional qualifications and replaces the
15 existing directives in the field of the recognition of professional
qualifications. It constitutes the first comprehensive modernization
of the regulations for professional mobility in over 40 years. The new
directive requires member states to facilitate the free movement of
doctors and recognize the diplomas, certificates and other evidence
of formal qualifications in medicine awarded by other member
states. Directive 2005/36/EC is thus the decisive directive for the
migration of physicians in the European Economic Area and provides for the automatic recognition of formal qualifications in
general and formal qualifications of specialized physicians in EU
member states. It provide the legal basis for all forms of mobility for
health professionals, whether they are establishing themselves per-
manently in another member state or simply providing services on an
occasional or temporary basis (Peeters et al. 2009; Zimmerman 2008).

One of the problems of the approach taken in the sectoral directives is that the details of the legislation require significant negotiation, making the legislative process slow and causing difficulties
whenever reforms are needed (Hervey and McHale 2004). As a
result, the ECJ was asked for clarification in cases such as *Van
Broeckmeulen*,[25] and ruled that the Dutch registration committee was
not allowed to require additional training for general practitioners
who had received their medical training abroad.

The ruling in *Van Broeckmeulen* prompted a directive (86/457/
EEC)[26] on specific training in general medical practice, which effectively overturned the Court's decision on *Van Broeckmeulen*. The directive recognizes general medical practice as a specialty and thus
allows member states to require additional training for general practitioners trained abroad. Despite this clarification, physicians continue to experience practical difficulties in having their qualifications
recognized in other member states. This creates a substantial number

of complaints to the Commission every year (Hervey and McHale 2004). While aggrieved practitioners can take their complaints to the ECJ or ask the Commission to intervene, the practical result is that member states can maintain tight control over professionals. If there is an influx of foreign doctors or nurses, as there was in the UK in the early 2000s, it is because the member state wanted it.

PUBLIC HEALTH

Public health has a long history in EU law, mostly as a suspect exception to EU principles such as non-discrimination and more recently as a response to crises in the food supply. It also enjoys a constituency within health care, unlike most health policies that the EU has produced. That constituency is made up of public health advocates who seek funding and support for their interventions and policies, often because of their frustration at the member state level. The result has been a sector with increasingly deep and strong connections between policy advocates and their sponsoring DGs (usually DG Sanco). First, this shows up mostly in networks surrounding the European Centre for Disease Prevention and Control (ECDC) and forums, such the Platform on Diet, Nutrition and Physical Activity. The Platform is a perfect case of the ambiguity of politics: born out of a shared concern about obesity and physical inactivity, it incorporates actors as distinct as McDonald's and the European Heart Forum. The goal is to explore ways to solve the problems without legislation, which suits companies whose products make people fat, because they avoid legislation and such pressure, and which suits many advocates, because it raises the profile of their issue and because serious EU anti-obesity legislation is unlikely in the current liberalizing climate anyway (Greer and Vanhercke 2009).

Second, there is funding. The European Union has been increasingly open to funding health groups and components of larger bids that focus on health. This is attractive to health organizations; a significant number of the lobbyists working on EU health issues are looking for grants and many lobbyists who do higher-level policy work justify themselves to their sponsors with their notices of new grants and assistance in writing bids. The most relevant funding is divided between DG Sanco and DG Research; the latter has a long history of cultivating connections with researchers, and the bio-medical research establishment is an obvious constituency for it to develop.

Third, there are specific areas of EU responsibility. Probably the most important is blood and blood products regulation. This was born of social spillover. As the BSE ('mad cow') disease developed, it became evident that the EU market in animals and animal products was extensive and created opportunities for weak regulation or a disease outbreak to create problems for other member states. It led to the inclusion in the Maastricht Treaty of an EU competency for blood and blood products as a warrant against future such episodes (Faber 2004; Farrell 2005). While that might not be the allocation of competencies that makes sense, it does make sense if we view it as a decision by member states to solve one problem (BSE) without creating a broad new EU competency. The politics of blood in the EU are a small but perfect example of EU methods: the EU model in blood was to create a network of responsible member-state blood regulators (thereby shifting the centre of gravity of blood policy from the Council of Europe, a wholly separate organization, to the EU). This meant creating a similar infrastructure in each member state – leading to the Europeanization of previously distinct policy fields.

One of the most far-reaching developments, and one of the least studied, is the Europeanization of communicable disease control. The combination of EU-level resources in the Stockholm-based European Centre for Disease Prevention and Control (with the acronym ECDC, a nod to the United States' Centres for Disease Control), an internal market in areas such as agriculture with both zoonoses (animal-borne diseases)and EU law trumping borders, and wide divergence in the public health capacity of different member states all created a field for progressive Europeanization (Rowland 2006).

PUBLIC PROCUREMENT

A key part of EU internal market regulation involves creating 'fair' markets that do not give undue advantages to firms from one member state or unduly privilege the public over private sectors. Implementing this goal has given rise to the large bodies of law dealing with competition, state aids and public procurement (Prosser 2005, 2009).

Public procurement law is the impressive edifice of regulations and procedures created to make sure that the public sector purchasers of the different EU member states do not discriminate in favour of domestic suppliers – that German car manufacturers could bid to supply the French police, or that French computer makers could bid to supply Italian government offices. It is a complicated, albeit routinized fact of public sector life in Europe, with the basic requirements for small bids being transparency and larger bids requiring advertisements in the *Official Journal of the European Communities* and procedures to make discrimination harder.

In this basic sense, public procurement is nothing new, and neither are its little complications. A nice, simple example came with oxygen tanks in the UK. Procurement under EU laws is slower than older NHS procurement systems and turned out to mean changing suppliers, and so NHS facilities that used a lot of oxygen had to buy larger storage tanks in order to accommodate longer periods between purchases of oxygen (Silio 2001). It is to be hoped that the greater transparency and possible competition outweighed the deadweight costs of new oxygen tanks.

The larger threat comes from its interaction with the multiplicity of purchaser–provider divides across the EU. It is common, in many different ways, for EU health systems to contract for some health care services with the private sector, but not to operate full markets, with some services not tendered, or subsidies attached to some services, or any manner of uncompetitive bids accepted in order to facilitate cross-subsidies. This is particularly common in the many systems with mixed public–private systems, with some services exposed to public–private competition but others generally sent to public sector facilities in order to keep them functioning.

The problem is that many systems' pragmatic use of markets, or subsidies to private and semi-public operators, looks idiosyncratic and discriminatory to EU public procurement law. Once there is a market, EU public procurement law is generally hostile to exceptions despite the fact that the member states have been invited to enumerate in Annex III of Directive 2004/18/EC[27] national bodies to be considered contracting entities for the purpose of EU public procurement law. In *Tögel*,[28] the ECJ ruled that the public procurement rules apply to social security institutions when they contract with service providers even when they offer benefits in nature and even when such benefits include auxiliary services of commercial nature (Hatzopoulos 2005). In *Ambulanz Glöckner*,[29] the ECJ held that cross-subsidy between tendered and other services was legitimate.

One way of reading the two cases together is to accept that the Court does not intervene directly in the precise way the states organize health care services, but rather oversees that the system chosen by each state is applied in accordance with the Treaty rules.

(Hatzopoulos 2005: 162)

STATE AIDS AND COMPETITION LAW

It is in competition law and state aids that the interaction of policy – especially liberalizing policy – and EU law is most unpredictable and prone to cause problems (Thomson and Mossialos 2009). The organization of health care systems in all EU member states relies on various systems of cross-subsidization between different public, semi-public and private bodies and on a network of agreements and contracts between these bodies. In order to ensure the proper functioning of their health care systems and to promote general social policy objectives, a certain degree of state planning and financing is indispensable (Hatzopoulos 2009) and the member states have thus frequently seen the need to inject money into entities operating in the health care sector (Hatzopoulos 2005).

One frequently cited example of health care organizations caught in this regulatory jungle are public hospitals (Hatzopoulos 2009: 150). Based on the rulings of the ECJ in *Geraets-Smits and Peerbooms* and *FENIN*,[30] the more integrated into a national health system a provider of health care services is, the less likely it is to be considered an undertaking subject to the rules on state aids as specified in Articles 87 to 89 EC. Naturally, private hospitals have long opposed state aids for their public competitors. In *Asklepios Kliniken*,[31] the applicant, a private German hospital company, requested a Commission investigation of allegedly incompatible state aid to public hospitals in Germany. The request was denied on the grounds that the Commission was entitled to spend time investigating the complaint, especially as it reasonably waited for the outcome of the then pending *Altmark* case.[32]

In its judgment in *Altmark*, the ECJ eventually held that subsidies given to an undertaking for the accomplishment of certain services of general interest may not constitute state aid, provided the so-called Altmark conditions are met.[33] The Commission extended the Court's rulings in *Altmark* by adopting the Altmark Decision (Commission Decision 2000/842/CE),[34] which provides for a number of block exemptions from the state aids rules where the Altmark conditions are not met. In its Altmark Decision, the Commission admits that moneys given to hospitals for fulfilling their public service obligations qualify as state aids but are deemed compatible with the internal market and need not be notified to the Commission. As a result, the arguments now are about processes for defining public service obligations, services of general and general economic interests, and whether markets can be rolled back, i.e. once a service is open to ordinary competition between commercial undertakings, can it be closed again?

OPEN METHOD OF CO-ORDINATION AND NEW GOVERNANCE

The Open Method of Co-ordination (OMC) has possibly the most disproportionate ratio of academic writing to practical effect of anything in the EU (for good reviews, see Borras and Jacobsson 2004; Dehousse 2004; Wincott 2002, 2003). The OMC is a peer-review process. Member states agree desirable goals (equitable, quality, accessible, financially sustainable health care) and indicators, produce 'National Action Plans' identifying weaknesses and policies that will remedy them, and then present them to each other and discuss. It is an example of a broad set of instruments of 'new governance' that try to harness networks to produce policy outcomes without hierarchical imposition.

In health, the relevant OMC is the 'Social Protection Committee' and it is serviced by DG Employment and Social Affairs. It is that DG's major beachhead in health policy, and some interviewees saw it as a useful forum in which to make statements about member state priorities that might influence the Court (Greer and Vanhercke 2009).

Participating in the OMC is not especially difficult, although it has contributed to rationalization of information flows in a few states; most OMC reports read like little more than condensed versions of the country reports of the European Observatory on Health Systems and Policies, leavened with government statements of priorities. The questions are whether the issues raised in OMCs affect member state policies, whether the process affects policymaking within member states, or whether learning from the OMC process influences policy. In many cases the governments that are most capable of developing health policy are the least interested in the OMC; one British official used a well-known Whitehall and NHS phrase for politically inspired bureaucratic busywork when he called it 'feeding the beast' in October 2008. But it is methodologically difficult to identify its effects across the EU, and some (such as educating member state officials) are rather indirect. The most important effect of the OMC and other state forums is that they allow member states to make detailed statements about their preferences and image of health services. They might thereby deter the European Court of Justice from making increasingly intrusive and detailed interventions.

FURTHER ISSUES

This is an impressive, and impressively complicated, list of issues. So are the issues not discussed here. They include pharmaceuticals, which has an extensive regulatory and market access regime on the EU level, with its own tensions: between member state pricing and EU markets, between consumer interests and company interests, and between different sectors (Hauray 2006; Mossialos et al. 2001; Permanand 2006). They also include medical devices regulation, which is similar and also has been Europeanized for longer than health care services or public health policy (Altenstetter 2005). Furthermore, eHealth, which involves major issues of data protection and IT business interests, is also a major issue with high stakes. I exclude them because, as a practical question, they are already in different policy worlds.

Then there are other policies and issues that influence health outcomes without coming from health systems. Some are policies that influence health outcomes: while almost any part of any budget has a health impact, it is particularly hard to deny that environmental health and occupational safety measures do not affect health. They also, of course, apply to health systems; for years, Europe's health care organizations have had to comply with them and other standards.

CONCLUSION

The key fact about these policies is that they all come from different places: different institutional homes, different policy debates, different bodies of law, different lobbies and different sets of experts. Some, such as the public health or quality agendas, cater to incumbent health policymakers and might attract them to Europe. Others, such as state aids and competition law, apply not just legal instruments but a whole style of politics developed far from the health policy world.

So as of yet there is no European Union health 'policy'. There are policies of the European Union, and some of them, in a combination not yet determined, will shape the health systems of the EU states. But all of them increasingly mean that the European Union, however fragmented, is a fact and a strategic challenge for health policymakers. Segregating the different policy areas, whether in sections of this chapter or in the edited books that are the foundation of the topic, is legally coherent but does not map onto the lived experience of the EU's health policy 'patchwork' (Hervey and Vanhercke 2009). No matter how different the law of state aids may be from the promotion of EU cancer care, those who represent parts of health systems, be they health lobbyists or member states, need to engage with the issues and respond to them.

If nothing else, member states often ask why they are filling out essentially the same questionnaire multiple times. The Open Method of Co-ordination, legislative consultations, DG Sanco consultations and presidency conferences on comparative health policy all come from different parts of the EU political world, are expected to build the capacity and reach of different networks, and are part of different political agendas, but end in very similar questionnaires that the same French, German, Spanish or UK official is obliged to fill out.

The EU always matters when it is doing what it does best – regulatory law and legislation. But implementation, the consequences of its policies, and the effects of its pronouncements and effects such as the OMC vary. They vary with the likelihood that the member state or its lobbies influenced the EU policy. That brings us to the politics behind and around these policies.

NOTES

1 The key work on health systems and the EU nowadays is Mossialos et al. (2009). The work that covers a broader range of public health issues as well is Steffen (2005). A shorter review that focuses on internal market law is Dawson and Mountford (2008). Older and highly influential works that trace the evolution of both the EU policies, and the debates surrounding them, are Busse et al. (2002), Hervey and McHale (2004), McKee et al. (2002), Mossialos and McKee (2002).

2 As a lobbyist noted in 2006, playing off the fact that social security co-ordination is still built around freedom of movement of labour: 'They have gone as far as you can go with 1408/71 and the EHIC. Now it is about making the model for citizens as opposed to workers'.

3 *Kohll* v. *Union des Caisses de Maladie* Case C-158/96 [1998].
4 *Decker* v. *Caisse de Maladie des Employees Prives* C-120/95 [1998].
5 It was a colleague of Yves Jorens who physically threw it away; see Jorens' comment at the European Health Management Association conference on 30 March 2007, Brussels.
6 Referring to this 1991 decision (*Grogan*) one particularly farsighted hospital lobbyist said 'That is when we first discovered we are a service. It did not say anything about us, but we are logical'.
7 *Vanbraekel* v. *Alliance National des Mutualites Chretiennes* (ANMC) C-368/98 [2001].
8 *Geraets-Smits* v. *Stichting Ziekenfonds VGZ, Peerbooms* v. *Stichting CZ Groep Zorgverzekeringen* C-157/99 [2001]
9 *Mueller-Faure* v. *Onderlinge Waarborgmaatschappij OZ Zorgverzekeringen UA, van Riet* v. *Onderlinge Waarborgmaatschappij ZAO Zorgverzekeringen* C-385/99 [2003].
10 *Watts* v. *Bedford Primary Care Trust and Secretary of State for Health* C-372/04 [2006].
11 However, member states' powers to regulate medical practice would have prevented some of the worst imaginable abuses, as discussed under 'Professional Mobility'.
12 A Green Paper is an exploratory document on policy options, following the UK usage.
13 Talking of a forum they organized, a member state medical lobbyist said in 2006: 'They [bring together] health ministry officials. Not DG Internal Market zealots, [who are] free single market people'.
14 Directive 93/104/EC OJ 1993 L 307/18.
15 Directive 2003/88/EC OJ 2001 L 299/9.
16 *Sindicato of Médicos of Asistencia Pública (SiMAP)* C-303/98 [2000].
17 *Jaeger* C-151–02 [2003].
18 Slightly lower estimates of the required number of full-time equivalent physicians can be found in Zimmermann (2008) who states that 18,700 new physicians as well as 10,900 administrative and other personnel would need to be recruited by German hospitals to comply with the Working Time Directive.
19 Interview, German hospitals association, Berlin, June 2008.
20 Directive 2000/34/EC OJ 2000 L 195/41.
21 Directive 75/362/EEC OJ 1975 L 167/1.
22 Directive 75/363/EEC OJ 1975 L 167/14.
23 Directive 93/16/EEC OJ 1993 L 165/1.
24 Directive 2005/36/EC OJ 2005 L 255/22.
25 *Van Broeckmeulen* C-246/80 [1981] ECR 2311.
26 Directive 86/457/EEC OJ 1986 L 267/26, subsequently amended by Directive 2001/19/EC.
27 Public Procurement Directive 2004/18/EC.
28 *Tögel* C-76/97 [1998] ECR I-5357.
29 *Ambulanz Glöckner* C-475/99 [2001] ECR I-8089.

30 *Federación Española de Empresa de Tecnología Sanitaria (FENIN)* v. *Commission of the European Communities* C-205/03.
31 *Asklepios Kliniken* v. *Commission EUECJ* T-167/04 [2004].
32 *Altmark* C-280/00.
33 The Altmark conditions state that, first, the recipient undertaking must actually have public service obligations to discharge, and the obligations must be clearly defined. Second, the parameters on the basis of which the compensation is calculated must be established in advance in an objective and transparent manner. Third, the compensation cannot exceed what is necessary to cover all or part of the costs incurred in the discharge of the public service obligations, taking into account the relevant receipts and a reasonable profit. Finally, where the undertaking which is to discharge public service obligations, in a specific case, is not chosen pursuant to a public procurement procedure which would allow for the selection of the tenderer capable of providing those services at the least cost to the community, the level of compensation needed must be determined on the basis of an analysis of the costs which a typical undertaking, well run and adequately provided with means of transport, would have incurred.
34 The lobbying behind this package created some strange bedfellows, with hospitals and social housing operators discovering their common interests as public service organizations.

4

DOING SOMETHING ABOUT IT

The EU, as much as disease regimes, obesity, financing, ageing or communicable disease, is a major strategic challenge facing Europe's health systems. Submitting to a new and poorly defined regulatory system is always a challenge, one that will influence the capacity of health systems to fulfil new or old goals as diverse as equity and quality.

Responding requires strategic leadership and political direction. That is not just because adapting complex and slow-changing health systems to EU regulation is difficult; it is also because the framework of EU health policy is being developed now. The health systems and member states that can influence the policy framework now will be the ones that can reduce transition and compliance costs, avoid distorted priorities, and even use EU health policy to good ends in the future. Influence now, when the EU is developing its basic framework, will shape the costs and benefits to taxpayers and patients later (Greer 2008a).

WHAT WORKS IN EU POLITICS

The European Union is a phenomenally complex policymaking system. The principal strategic challenge is to be able to see how to advance or oppose a given idea across many forums, some of them formal and easily identifiable (such as Council or European Parliament votes) and some of them nebulous and of doubtful value (as with the endless round of seminars and conversations in Brussels, which are collectively influential but individually often waste time). How does a stakeholder or government identify a developing idea or policy of interest, gauge its likelihood of success, and then develop a strategy to promote it or suppress it across the many venues in which policy is made?

The challenge is great because of the complexity of timing and participation in EU politics. First, timing is difficult to predict, and often events cannot be predicted. The EU is, like many political systems, an unstable combination of extremely long-term and extremely short-term planning (Kingdon 1995; Mazey and Richardson 1995); a week is a long time in politics but a year flies by. Proposals (such as on Services of General Economic Interest or Patient Mobility) can be planned for years and then be suddenly amended or delayed; politicians (such as German Chancellor Angela Merkel) enter office to discover that their EU presidency was planned out years before by officials, but also broker last-minute deals between heads of state; and meetings stuck at an impasse on any level suddenly yield to a new proposal. Effectiveness not only requires adaptability to such elastic timetables, but also requires understanding both institutions and the politics behind them. When are the conditions right for a given proposal? When does a problem line up with a workable policy idea and a group of politicians (or member states, or Commission officials) who are interested in pushing it through? Being too early or too late means being irrelevant, and that often means that influence must be not just tightly targeted but also well timed. The EU's rigid timetabling, such as Commission work plans, also drives much activity. The result is not just to force member states to speed up their policymaking in many cases, and to make their elites discuss issues they might prefer to ignore; it is also to create challenges for all those in the secret garden who were used to more control over the timing and agenda-setting of health politics.

Second, the complexity and interaction of multiple arenas means that the scope of engagement can vary wildly. One of the key facts about any political situation is the scope of engagement, i.e. who is involved (Schattschneider 1960[1975])? In the secret garden of health policy the scope of engagement was generally narrow and stable; it is a commonplace of health politics that it involves constant, close interaction between states and a few large interest groups that are often engaged in governance activities on behalf of the state. In the public park of EU health policy, there are a few regulars; member state officials who know what events to attend and how to interact, and equally skilled lobbyists from a few organizations. They form the basis of the developing European Union health policy community, and there is something of a circuit of events they attend. But there is an enormous shifting cast of interested ministries, ministers, DGs, politicians and lobbies that enter and leave the field. That wide and unstable scope of engagement increases the information require-ments needed to be effective and increases the likelihood of a surprise – which means that it is good to be nimble.

Information (and imagination)

Much of the analysis of EU policymaking requires good imagin-ation because it involves so many unknowns:

- First, what is likely to become of a developing EU policy? For example, when the Commission first began to speak of EU 'Centres of References' for rare diseases, what were the odds that member states led by Germany and France would succeed (as they did) in transforming the proposal into one calling for 'networks of reference', a shift that allows the networks to belong to single member states rather than be Europe-wide and involve the Commission.
- Second, how will a policy idea be interpreted in EU law? For example, what were the odds that the Working Time Directive would be interpreted by the Court as it was in *SiMAP* and *Jaeger*? Or what are the chances now that the Court, or a domestic court interpreting EU law, will interpret law on state aids so as to ban the subsidies that keep most German hospitals afloat?
- Third, then, how can the policy be implemented within each mem-ber state? For example, it is quite likely that the Working Time Directive's application to junior doctors has led to a rash of lying by hospital managers.
- Fourth and finally, then, given all those unknowns, what will be the impact of a given EU policy on things that really matter such as the efficiency, cost, quality, universality and solidarity of the health systems it would affect?

Given these four layers of unknowns, it is not surprising that we often know little about EU policies – as seen in health policymakers' collective failure to predict the likely effects of the WTD or the legal obviousness of the patient mobility decisions.[1] What is surprising is that member states and stakeholders often do know quite a lot about the effects of prospective policies. Much of what member states know comes from the skills of their own ministries' health depart-ments and reflects their hiring decisions. But other than the qualities of individual officials (which is not happenstance; every member state has clever officials, but not all of them assign them to health or EU health affairs), the structurally important issue is the ability of health ministries to draw on both the EU knowledge and the knowledge of health systems required to work through these questions. In other words, that means the networks that the ministerial officials use to develop their impact analysis. If the health ministry does not develop those networks, it is unlikely that anybody else in a given government will do it.

Co-ordination

In general, co-ordination is thought to be a good thing (the best reviews and comments are in Bogdanor 2005; Jordan and Schout 2006; Wright 1996). The basic division, in practice, is between active, passive and no co-ordination. No co-ordination means acting independently and hoarding information, passive co-ordination is responding to requests and active co-ordination means trying to identify situations in which co-ordination with another actor might be relevant.

For lobbies, it usually means co-ordination between member state, regional and EU organizations or branches; as Chapter 5 will discuss, this is necessary if any group is to be effective. That is not just because EU lobbies and member state organizations have complementary skills; it is often because the most effective route to influence EU policy is by lobbying a member state in its capital. The main problem is that European federations, and many EU lobbyists, are entrepreneurs who promote European integration, and their own operations, while many member state organizations are still quite parochial. Communication and trust problems can arise between them. Secondarily, the problem for EU-level organizations is that agreeing a meaningful position between 27 more or less capable and interested member state organizations can be very difficult.

For governments, it is often harder to co-ordinate. Co-ordination means that governments do not pursue contradictory policies. For example, all states faced a co-ordination problem with the proposal of the Services Directive, which economics ministries often supported but which health ministries generally sought to amend. It also means that coordinated governments are more effective negotiators; they can organize larger package deals in which they trade off less important priorities in some areas in order to pursue more important goals in others. It is, finally, good for democratic accountability.

In health, co-ordination is more important – and more problematic

– than those simple arguments suggest because so much EU health policy comes from 'adjacent' areas such as competition or labour law. Co-ordination can allow health policymakers to interject their concerns into debates about adjacent areas, or allow rival ministries and groups to impose their interpretations on health.

Finally, there is the basic problem of coping with the famous tendency of experts and advocates to (in Margaret Thatcher's terms) 'go native' in Brussels. For member states, the problem is that their experts might diverge from their strategy. The genius of European institutions, from the point of view of supporters of integration, is that the 'peculiar functional division of labour that exists between the Commission and the Union Council . . . triggers unique centrifugal forces at the very heart of national governments' (Egeberg 2006: 1). The logic is simple: if experts or government officials go to an EU function with some substantive goal, such as reducing obesity, or improving cancer care, or getting a grant, they might start to identify with the EU networks and what they can do, rather than the interest of their member state (which might seem abstract, or distant, or wrong, or which might appear to sacrifice a good end such as cancer care to some nebulous concept of sovereignty). The term, a neologism in French, is *engrenage* and it means to be 'geared into' the EU (Shore 2000, 2007). EU specialists working for member states are probably the only significant group who understand EU politics and are not advocates of the EU or its policies.

For lobbies, the problem is simpler: while most EU lobbyists must often lobby backwards to keep their members happy and engaged, there is also a temptation for them to lobby for what they know best, which is the EU. Ideally, an EU lobby membership or EU office is part of a coherent strategy spread across multiple levels. All too often, what we actually find is a more or less freelance lobbyist working to expand the place of a given issue on the EU agenda, which does serve that interest, but not necessarily in an efficient way or one that preserves the division of labour.

Nimbleness

Nimbleness is a desirable attribute in many kinds of politics; given the importance of timing, and the ways politics change when the scope of participation changes, it is a poor politician who cannot adapt quickly to changed circumstances. So, for example, the United Kingdom would not have been well served to go on insisting, after the *Watts* case went to the European Court of Justice, that there was no EU health competency. Instead, it used its presidency to develop the statement about values that emphasizes the role of member states.

Member states, being bureaucracies, have a difficult time; there is something of a contradiction in efforts to build a nimble bureaucracy.[2] The question for member states is whether their formal structures create either a highly responsive network (desirable but difficult); or have a component of hierarchy that allows somebody at the top to make fast decisions when circumstances change; or have the combination of fragmentation and bureaucratization that gives so much public administration a bad name.

One effect of systems that are not nimble is, quite literally, failure to show up. Some of the member states have poor records of even turning up, or voting, in the Council; both Germany and France have had this problem when they have not been able to sort out their internal co-ordination processes in time. Greater failure is hard to imagine, even if many of those votes were not very important.

Among lobbies, the co-ordination problems of European Union federations can impede nimbleness. They have to represent, usually, a number of member state organizations. The need to accurately represent their views (which often requires education about the issue) can make them very slow to react to EU policies. That, in turn, is why more engaged organizations can find it rational to hire their own EU representation.

Activity

Finally, effectiveness depends on activity. Member states usually manage to make it to Council meetings with a position, but that is a fairly minimal, passive, role. It is also one that is likely to leave member states voting on proposals that were, for all practical purposes, written by other people. The antidote is activity, meaning constant engagement with policymaking in Brussels as well as with the health system of the member state. That creates networks, builds information, and thereby allows the member state to influence agendas with credible, timely and often informal arguments.

Much of this activity is, necessarily, wasted. One UK official spent months working out the likely effect of the Services Directive on the NHS systems – work that obviously went to waste after Article 23 (health) was removed from the directive. Attendance at any given meeting or part might be a waste of time. But there are limits to anybody's ability to work out which activity will be wasted. Effectiveness, if not efficiency, means erring on the side of activity.

Activity is, however, complex. Many groups from a member state might be active as well as the member state itself; the UK NHS systems are represented by (at a minimum) the UK state, three devolved governments and the NHS Confederation, which is an association of NHS organizations. Arguably, the UK medical, nursing and other professional associations and UK citizens involved in a variety of EU associations are also representing the UK. So member states do not have a monopoly on activity, and in some cases they are less active and informed than their regional governments or lobbies.

CONCLUSION

the challenge for Europe is to attract the imagination of certain individuals. You need a certain mindset to enjoy that work. Plenty don't have it.

(Member state official, March 2006)

The challenge for anybody who would influence EU health policies is not hard to state (and not even all that novel, either): be informed, co-ordinated, nimble and active across all levels, with lobbies obviously most likely to be effective at the deliberative level, and the member states enjoying the opportunity to work across all three (or eschew organization and information and try to use their weight at the diplomatic level). Information, co-ordination, nimbleness and activity are probably desirable properties for activists and politicians anywhere, but they are certainly very important in the public park of the EU, where the natural complexity of Council voting rules or the mammoth European Parliament, or the tics of EU language (such as saying 'the country I know best' to refer to one's native member state) are actually dwarfed by the complexity of half a dozen DGs with different policy agendas and an effectively unlimited number of actors, ideas and policy problems from 27 different countries. It is to those actors, first lobbies and then member states, that the following chapters turn.

NOTES

1 In other words, the EU is an exogenous shock to health systems. The EU law that is being applied to health is established in other fields, and the health decisions are not very intellectually interesting in terms of EU law. But the mere fact that the decisions are endogenous to EU law is

compatible with them being exogenous to health. The earthquake might be endogenous to the fault line, but it is exogenous to the city on top.

2   The volume of writings on this topic in management literature is staggering. Presumably this means it is not a problem confined to the public sector.

5

LOBBIES

Most people who engage with the EU act, whether they accept the label or not, as lobbyists and policy advocates. When the UK's Royal College of Nursing sends delegations to a Brussels meeting on patient mobility, when experts gather to send a representation to the Commission on pending legislation, when a part-time staffer is hired to follow EU grant opportunities and make relevant contacts, when an association joins an EU-level body in order to promote its interests, or when a group hires an EU policy officer to keep track of developments, they are lobbying.

Lobbying is often seen as a rather foreign practice, with professional lobbyists often seen as arising in France, Germany and Spain only in recent decades (Bandelow 2007; Grossman and Saurugger 2004), and the vast, intense EU lobbying scene in Brussels sometimes presented as a sort of anomaly.[1] The very fact of the lobby reflects the looser articulation between the EU and its diverse societies; the Commission and Parliament need information about the very diverse polity they govern, while for lobbies the EU affords a range of opportunities that call for hiring specialists in EU politics (Mazey and Richardson 1995). In short, the oligopolies of power and influence often found in domestic health politics cannot be sustained in the context of the EU. The lobby is a creature of the public park, and supersedes the webs and entwined networks of the garden.

The secret garden of health has been particularly hostile to explicit lobbying in many countries. Relatively stable constellations of interests, medical professions above all, dominated politics and influence often worked through insider channels. This is not the case in the EU, where there is no reason why any given group – professional, organizational, or national – need be heard. They must organize, through a variety of means including participation in EU-level forums and establishment of their own Brussels offices, if they are to influence EU policy.

The rise of lobbying in EU health policy is a demonstration of the way that the EU is expanding into health care as well. On the one hand, the development of EU health policies in areas such as patient mobility, professional mobility and working times all create challenges and opportunities for health policymakers and advocates. Even if member state organizations wish to defend the status quo, the way to do that is by engaging with the EU. So it pays for groups as diverse as the German Techniker Krankenkasse (a social insurance fund), the European Heart Forum and the NHS Confederation, which represents the management of UK health service organization, to engage their own professional lobbyists, while a wide variety of organizations from across Europe join EU-wide associations that engage in such debates.

On the other hand, the attractiveness and power of the EU does not just lie in its regulatory power. It also lies in its networks – the forums it offers for advocates to make their case for different health policy initiatives, to share experiences, to meet up, and to speak with policymakers. And it lies in the famous grants, which are a miniscule amount of money by most standards (the entire EU budget is 1.1 per cent of the EU's GDP) but which are 'new money' and thereby attract far more interest than the absolute sums would suggest.

Whether it is in pursuit of grants, or influence, or visibility, or even just defensive action against potentially problematic EU law, many organizations have found it worthwhile to engage with the EU. While many prefer to work through their member state, enough have found it important to work on their own to compensate for disagreements with their governments or failings in their member states' abilities to influence. These incentives, and the efforts of established EU lobbyists to explain the importance of what they do, have brought many organizations into Brussels politics in other areas. Health lobbying is still in its infancy, but it should grow because of both the size of the health sector (which can, collectively, afford quite a few lobbyists) and because of the potential stakes. Even if their aims are defensive, the rise of those lobbyists increases the size and visibility of the EU health policy arena whose existence was denied not long ago.

EU LOBBYING

Brussels is, by most accounts, the second most lobbied capital city in the world, and is not far behind Washington, DC in the sheer number of lobbyists (though its relatively weak registration system also means that a definitive count of lobbyists is harder to achieve than in the United States) (Greenwood 2003). The functional argument for lobbying is that it is necessary because the EU suffers from a permanent, structural, information deficit. Neither the Commission, nor the Court, nor the (large but weakly resourced) European Parliament can understand the effects of what they are doing or identify beneficial initiatives. The Commission has enough staff to build networks and support, and to identify areas of potential EU action, but nowhere near enough to understand the complex issues at stake across Europe, particularly in an area such as health care.

The result is that good EU lobbyists are the ones who specialize in finding, (re)packaging and sharing important information with each other, in order to identify opportunities to influence, in order to shape agendas and framing, and in order to communicate with policymakers and shape their decisions. This can take a variety of forms. Some are mundane, for example standing to speak at public gatherings and prefacing a remark with a long statement about the name and large membership (i.e. credibility) of the organization. Some are small but effective; the Standing Committee of European Doctors has a chief executive from Luxembourg, which made it easier to suggest patient safety to the Luxembourg government as a theme for its presidency. Some are simply dramatic: the large protests against the proposed Services Directive, which included a group of French electricians who cut off the electricity to Commissioner Bolkestein's holiday home (Buck and Bickerton 2005), were part of the same campaign that had lobbyists arguing for the exclusion of health from the directive. Some are benign – briefing members and then bringing them to Brussels harnesses not only their expertise but also the thirst of many European (and other) politicians for somebody from 'the real world'. Most often, they take the form of a quiet word with an influential person at the earliest stages, and providing information later, for example, to MEPs when there is legislation. A good lobbyist understands and operates as many levers of power as possible, which means gaining access to people by providing what (information) they need. This is not the same thing as public affairs, or 'spin doctoring', which is also done in Brussels but which is less important because public opinion is less important. One top lobbyist, who had experience in both EU lobbying and corporate public affairs, observed that lobbyists tend to be free with information because 'it is a chit that you trade and that you use to be credible . . . but in public affairs information is a weapon'.

The trade of the lobbyist, in that sense, is quite simple: identify the most influential people and make a case attuned to their interests.[2] This means understanding the institutional basics. It also means understanding the complex interconnections between member-state level and EU-level politics; for example, lobbying a member state government is not just a way to influence its stance in the Council, but can also influence 'its' Commissioner and that person's Cabinet. Often, this comes from buying into a network; one lobbyist commented that while the presentational skills and technical knowledge of a lobbyist are limited, over time 'the people you know get more important'. Knowing the levers and people, the skills for which organizations hire lobbyists, also means knowing how to appeal to them. For example, proposing an initiative to do with pharmaceuticals will be a different operation when one is addressing DG Enterprise (whose principal engagement with health is the promotion of pharmaceutical industry interest) or when one is addressing DG Sanco (which is connected to broader health policy communities but is weaker than Enterprise in the Commission hierarchy).

Likewise, the European Parliament, which constantly gains importance, is a distinctive world of its own. Some lobbies, especially narrower ones such as disease groups, have been successful setting up and servicing cross-party 'Eurogroups' of MEPs with a special interest. Eurogroups are often inactive, but they can be a very effective way of drawing attention to an issue so that it can be included in policy decisions. Member states and regional governments, in the same spirit, stay in contact with and try to supply information to 'their' MEPs in order to influence them, while the biggest and most inclusive lobbies will try to communicate to as many MEPs as possible while building relationships with the ones who are specializing on the issue (in the way that John Bowis MEP specialized in, and made himself key to, health services policy).

Credibility matters greatly: credibility as a representative of a significant social interest, credibility as a source of useful information and credibility as a person. This is not always easy to establish by interviewing a lobby directly. A transcript of an interview with a lobbyist whose organization is generally seen as ineffective, or which is about to break up, or that is about to lose its funding, will often look like one from a successful lobby. They all have working committees to represent member organizations between annual meetings, circulate papers through those committees, and use their lobbyist to both collect anticipatory information and then find the right way to put their case privately to officials, semi-publicly at events, or even publicly with a press campaign.

So how do we identify a credible lobby? Part of the hierarchy of lobbies can be established by looking at their activity; there are a number of groups (more than we would expect from pure chance) that engage with all forms of EU health policy engagement. They include well-known actors such as the European Public Health Alliance (EPHA) and European Health Management Association (EHMA). Part can be established, as I did, by asking most interviewees what groups matter to them. Part can be noted, if not proved, by looking at which lobbyists attend different meetings and how they are treated. I once (in 2007) watched a senior Commission official move around a room suggesting to influential lobbyists that they might want to help with an initiative that had run into trouble in the College of Commissioners by lobbying senior commissioners through their member states and Cabinets. That is a relatively high-level lobbying operation, and not one that is undertaken lightly or without deniability. It was interesting to see which lobbyists he picked out: they were the ones with personal and organizational track records as constructive (from his point of view), energetic (participating in multiple forums) and professional (by hiring experienced Brussels actors).

In that world, opening a Brussels office is not something that should be done lightly. By the standards of many organizations, it is expensive; renting European Quarter office space (often shared) and hiring a 20- or 30-something European politics specialist is costly. But more importantly, it is a statement. It says that an organization seeks and will pay the price to develop credibility. That is why UK NHS bodies initially chose to add an officer to existing regional offices rather than set up on their own. It is also why the decision of the NHS Confederation (a body of UK health management that purports to represent the NHS systems) to set up a full Brussels office was a dramatic statement. It is also why an incompetent, or intermittent, Brussels office might be worse than none. The EU health politics world divides into a small circuit of people who generally know each other and a large number of people who are for all purposes crashing the party. For organizations that cannot commit the resources to be serious Brussels players, it is better to make organized and informed entrances, or work through EU federations, than to set up a Brussels office that will make a splash, not develop much credibility, and vanish when the interest of the chief executives at home dissipates.

So EU lobbies cannot drift free of their member state members. A few well-known lobbies (as well as the more forgettable disease groups) are essentially one-person organizations, with industry or Commission funding and not much life outside Brussels. But most EU level organizations are federations of member state organizations, and are vastly smaller than member-state professional, patient or management associations that provide a wide range of services to many members, and have staffs and money to match. Some, such as the European hospital federation HOPE, must even manage a diverse membership of individual operators, associations, regional governments and member states. An EU federation is usually a lobbying operation with few member services. Likewise, the Brussels offices of member state health organizations are as a rule very small. The German TK fund has almost 11,000 employees, and one part-time EU lobbyist. The British Medical Association is a giant in UK health politics and has one person in Brussels.

They must also keep their member state and individual members happy since it is those members that pay the bills. One lobbyist stated the problems:

> In Brussels you work in a European way. You must be quite dynamic on a project of law or communication. You have to take a position quickly. I cannot ask for them to wait while all read it. . . . Your members – they take their time. They have other occupations. In Italy, they work in the Italian style. France, the French style. Our members are a bit old, 65 years old, all working in the same sector, many are professors or doctors. They are intelligent and open but this is not their domain.

Furthermore, not all of the most effective levers in EU politics are in Brussels. The Commission is in Brussels, and policy debates and deliberations happen there. Information is there. But after that, member state politics start to matter: the European Parliament is in Brussels, but the best way to an MEP might be through that person's member state. Member states themselves have Permanent Representations with health councillors who will meet lobbyists, but when I asked two of them in October 2008 interviews why lobbyists wish to speak with them, they both answered with the same phrase in two languages: 'I ask them that!' Counsellors in Permanent Representations can provide tactical advice to their home departments, but they usually cannot rewrite their instructions. And so even if the EU group knows what it wants, the member state association, which can influence the member state government, is the most effective influencer.

EU health lobbying is still young, and is often quite fragile. DGs' behaviour and Commission administration influences them: as Holly Jarman (personal communication) notes, American groups pay to lobby while the EU lobbies are paid to lobby. Consider one lobbyist's 2006 complaint:

> When it comes to policy, the Commission is quite complacent. It uses funding to NGOs that it thinks can do the Commissions work for them. Even when the funding is 80–100 per cent, the Commission are very bad payers – those groups survive on bank loans. The Commission doesn't – DG Sanco doesn't – have a very strong relationship with the health community . . . not as useful as DG Environment and its NGOs. So the result was no solidarity when Sanco needed help in the fight against Internal Market over the draft Services Directive.

A given organization will often have only one, and at most half a dozen, employees in Brussels. All the flaws of different kinds of groups matter; the EU organization for carers has had a harder time organizing itself than the EU organization that represents the aged despite similar starting points and help. Both are less effective, clearly, than bigger organizations such as the European Public Health Alliance and European Health Management Association, which are in turn smaller and more fragile than major pharmaceutical companies or EU lobbying giants such as IBM.

But lobbying is crucial: if the EU has any influence, then it pays to have a seat at the table. This means that more and more groups try to seek it, and once at the table develop ideas that draw in other groups. This is highly unfortunate for those who would prefer that there be no such table anywhere in Brussels. It is, though, how political spillover works.

The next step, then, is that the lobbyists lobby for EU policies, which is often inseparable for arguing for new powers. Once there is a European Cancer Patients Coalition office in Brussels, for example, its leaders make arguments such as this:

> Astonishingly, within the EU, there seems to be little political will to share and apply evenly the knowledge we do have on how to prevent, diagnose and treat cancer, and how to care for

patients. Europe seems to have no legal basis for this. This is comprehensible only if we consider that countries in the EU came together first of all to form a common market, but it remains incomprehensible, all the same, if one considers that good health is what people treasure most. Small wonder that most EU citizens feel far removed from their EU.

(Sundstreth and Woods 2008: 192)

Extending EU powers are yoked to reducing cancer deaths in a rhetorical move ubiquitous in EU health policy circles; it becomes 'astonishing' that member states did not create a health care competency; and political spillover continues.

Once the EU starts to act in health policy – in this case because of the ECJ – every other interest has cause to engage with EU health policy. And once they are engaged in EU health policy, many will try to formulate positive agendas, seek funding, and pursue their policy ideas at the EU level (and perhaps play more sophisticated games by co-ordinating with their member state organizations). The result? EU health politics.

WHO ARE THE HEALTH LOBBIES?

European societies of various sorts are nothing new and people with a shared interest in medicine or health hardly needed political integration to create a society. EU-level groups have been forming since before the EU existed, and while there are clear spikes in overall EU lobbying that match major expansions of its powers (especially the Single Market project that culminated in 1992), health has seen a steady trickle of new organizational starts over a century.

What is more interesting is the distribution of health lobbies. If the problem is to defend the autonomy of health systems, or at least recognition of their peculiarities, and tilt the EU playing field in favour of health instead of the single market, then part of the solution is to have people in Brussels who can gain access and credibility and skilfully articulate their concerns, whether to make clear the negative consequences of a particular proposal for a particular health care system, or to steer major documents such as the Commission's public health strategies toward the areas where it can have a positive impact. That would mean a distribution of lobbyists that would represent both incumbents and advocates of the broader public health policies often lacking in member states, and representation from across every EU member state. That situation only partially exists.

Brussels bypass?

The most common hope lodged in the EU, after the universal siren call of a grant, is probably that of influence for the frustrated. The EU offers a different stage, with different languages, networks and opportunities. To advocates of causes that repeatedly lose in their national capitals, the prospect of finding EU engagement in their issue, developing EU-supported networks, perhaps winning EU grants, and even participating in EU legislation that can influence their own member states might be intoxicating.

One group that we might obviously expect to support and drive EU health policies is the more aggressive group of private-sector operators. That does not mean the private sector overall. Most if not all EU countries have a supplementary private health service sector that provides services not covered by the public schemes, or that provides them in greater luxury, or that provide them to the public sector, or that are formally contractors but are for most purposes public sector (as with general practice in the UK). These groups are often as bound in with the existing systems as the public sector; the main concern of the Rome-based Union of European Private Hospitals (UEHP) when the draft Services Directive came out was to avoid being regulated as a business if their public competitors were not. Their lobbyist explained that they were often equivalent to, and financed like, the public sector, and their members in countries as different as Belgium and Italy could no more survive deregulation than could their public sector equivalents.

The beneficiaries would be the more aggressive operators such as UnitedHealth and Humana from the United States, Capio from Sweden, or BUPA from the UK and a range of lesser-known companies in fields such as radiology or well-known companies engaged in private finance initiatives (PFIs). All of them have an interest in developing as competitive providers and could benefit from subjection of health systems to public procurement, state aids and services law. But they have been close to invisible in EU debates. Some of this is hiding; given the general unpopularity of markets as an idea in EU health policy, it is rational for them to work (like the tobacco industry) through lobbying firms such as Cabinet Stewart or some of the Brussels think tanks, though they are also UEHP members. But interviewees of all sorts, from Commission to other lobbyists, do not report much activity by the people who might stand to gain most from liberalizing EU activity. Why are the most obvious beneficiaries not doing more?

The answer is simple: as a private health care executive said to me in 2007, 'Why would we?' Battering down resistance in a country like France or Belgium is vastly harder than taking the abundant market opportunities on offer in England or Madrid. The Dutch opened up their health insurance market, and insurers went there. If one government is inviting you to a lucrative market, it would be odd to instead try to enter a market with a hostile government that could use a wide range of regulatory and economic fields to make business difficult and profitless. They do not need the bypass – yet. As we have already seen with *BUPA* and *Asklepios*, and will probably see with private providers in the UK, when they lose they will often try to use EU law to prevent member states rolling back the scope of their market.

The 'Brussels bypass' argument is often most apparent in the case of public health advocates, who in every country face political problems. If the dominant structural interest in most health systems is medicine, public health is almost always a subordinate interest with advocates who have a hard time commanding resources or space on the agenda (Alford 1975; Greer 2009a). In some member states, such as the UK, there is a relatively strong public health function, with professional training, institutions and formal leadership, and a substantial critical literature that points out its relative lack of influence over the many areas of public policy that shape population health. In others, especially the post-communist and a few of the Mediterranean states, the process of building a public health infrastructure has not always advanced beyond basic communicable disease control. The EU public health strategy might have flaws from the point of view of some member states, but it is a significantly more ambitious document than emerges from some other member states, and EU action in areas such as tobacco control has gone far beyond some countries even while disappointing many advocates.

Defensive manoeuvres

EU health politics is, of course, not primarily about attractiveness to public health advocates. If it were, there would be much less activity in competition law and much more activity in tobacco control and 'Health In All Policies'. If it were, in fact, the EU would not be the regulatory, market-building set of institutions that it is nowadays. So the key question is whether those charged with managing today's universal health care systems will be able to represent their systems.

In other words, what about the dominant coalitions in most member state health politics, above all medical professions and the groups that represent hospitals? One pair of experts on EU lobbying sketched a future that might disturb the former landlords of the secret garden:

> While it may be that the European Union is uniquely open and accessible for those with clearly defined interests, those parts of European society that lack these organizational resources, or remain too embedded in national tradition, to match the stringent requirements for interest articulation, may find themselves excluded from the emerging European polity.
>
> (Coen and Dannreuther 2003: 272)

They might find themselves bypassed in Brussels, due to their own 'obstinacy' in using their old member-state channels when they should be plunging into EU health politics (Beyers 2002).

It is not hard to claim that professions are poorly represented at the EU level, as lobbying expert Justin Greenwood and a number of interviewees argued (Greenwood 2003: 124–148). Major divisions split medicine, such as that between doctors who see themselves as 'liberal professions' and those closer to the state. One former Standing Committee of European Doctors (CPME) officer made a stirring defence of the commonality of doctors, highlighting 'the common perspective that comes from seeing life and death', but that does not overcome divisions between doctors who see themselves as an independent 'liberal profession' and those that do not. Nursing representation at the EU level is less split than the enormous diversity of nursing professions would suggest, but that is due in good part to the decision of the UK's Royal College of Nursing to focus on building EU representation for nursing across Europe, and the infrastructure of nursing across Europe, by supporting the Standing Committee of Nurses of the EU (PCN).

The situation of doctors, already 'extremely badly represented' (said a lobbyist in October 2008) by what one medical lobbyist called 'a crazy number of groups' in 2006 deteriorated in the summer of 2008 when its peak association CPME lost the French, Spanish and Italian medical associations. As a CPME officer explained, 'Our power comes from speaking for 2 million European doctors. If we do not speak for all of them, we are nothing.' The conflict was about a typical EU-level problem; the three seceding medical associations sought weighted voting that would reflect their large size and resented being outvoted by a perceived coalition of northern states. That was, of course, a reflection of their poor lobbying within the CPME. Medicine and the professions in general are also rather poor at form- ing coalitions; 'Perhaps it's our doctors' arrogance', as a medical lobbyist said, but the doctors and to a lesser extent all the medical professions are low profile or absent from many coalitions.

While doctors have serious difficulties at the EU level, the develop- ing lobbying capacity of incumbent health system leaders is not so bad. First, the medical profession is not only represented by its peak organization (let alone the federations of 'liberal professions' that have sometimes limply claimed to represent it: Greenwood 2003). The British and German medical associations both have their own lobby- ists in Brussels, and groups as diverse as the French and Finnish doctors have made the initial steps required to matter, bringing trained and briefed groups of doctors to meetings with Commission officials and MEPs who were selected for their influence and issuing position papers that make arguments in calm and European (rather than 'parochial', i.e. member state) terms.

Second, the medical profession is not the same as health systems overall. EPHA and EHMA both have many members engaged in running health systems and are both prone to speak for 'health sys- tems' overall in terms of policy and system-wide thinking. Both have memberships with interests and goals that might not appeal to health ministers: EHMA also serves many members who wish to improve their management skills and runs an important annual aca- demic conference, while EPHA does work on trade policy and access to medicines that is far from the interests of many Europeans but important as public health. They are influential, visible and prone, for example, to publicly note inconvenient issues important to many health managers such as the organizational costs of new policies. Such organizations are small and therefore always fragile, but their names are credible, and it would be a daring or incompetent officer who directed them away from their important EU niche.

Third, on a quantitative measure, the professions are not doing badly (Greer et al. 2008). It would be hard to develop a reliable statement about the relative power of professions in each EU coun- try, and the extent to which they transfer that power over to the EU level, but there does not seem to be an obvious problem. The per- centage of medical professional organizations that affiliate to an EU group for most countries is about the same as the overall percentage of their professions in all fields that affiliate to an EU group. Only NGOs are more common, and many NGOs are disease groups with limited reach (and the political handicap of pharmaceutical company funding).

The southern (and eastern) questions

The tensions within CPME were emblematic of a larger geographical bias in EU health policy. Attending EU health policy events in Brussels and elsewhere gives a stark impression of who engages in EU health lobbying. German, British, Scandinavian and Benelux citizens are ubiquitous. Citizens of Eastern Europe and the Mediterranean countries are almost invisible. Is this impression true?

Studies of EU lobbying in other fields certainly suggest as much. Justin Greenwood speaks of the EU's 'Southern Question': to what extent is there a deficit in the representation of states in southern Europe (Greenwood 2002)? Comparisons of different countries find different propensities to lobby, with lobbying apparently second nature to pluralist UK organizations or self-governing Germans, but something of a new development for the French (e.g. Fairbrass 2003; V. Schmidt 2006).

With colleagues, I conducted a quantitative study of EU groups (Greer et al. 2008). The number of organizations from a given member state that join an EU-level association is a crude but telling indicator of their propensity to engage with Europe. This is because participation in an EU-level association is the main first step. Even sophisticated organizations with their own Brussels offices, such as the British and German medical associations, also belong to and work with EU-level associations.

The evidence is compelling: even controlling for the effects of wealth, population and receipt of EU funds (which increase the number of organizations joining EU-level health groups), there is a systematic bias towards German-speaking, Scandinavian, Benelux and British lobbies. Perhaps it is due to southern European statism, or weak civil society, or more or less innovative health system leadership, but it means that any anecdotal impression of British, Benelux and German dominance at meetings is borne out.

CONCLUSION

Lobbies are already common in EU health politics, and are likely to become more common as more actors in the health sector find that the relatively small investment required to operate in Brussels is proportional to the importance of the policy changes, and opportunities, that the EU can cause.

But lobbying is not something that everybody does equally, and it by no means correlates with a group's actual need for political solutions. Do German and UK doctors have a particular need for EU representation that leads them to both support the CPME and establish their own offices? Probably not. Is there a compelling policy reason for German-speaking, Scandinavian, Benelux and British Isles groups to join, support and probably lead most EU organizations in greater numbers than their colleagues from Eastern or Mediterranean Europe? Probably not. Is there probably a bias from the relative representation of northwestern Europe that might make future policy problems for Bulgaria or Spain? Probably. Does it matter if they are not represented? In so far as it means that they are absent at the deliberative stages when policy ideas are developing, and will have to make up lost ground later when the proposals are set, the coalitions formed, and compliance potentially costly and damaging.

NOTES

1   For the major works on EU lobbying, see Beyers et al. (2009), Coen (2007), Coen and Richardson (2009), Mahoney (2008), Mazey and Richardson (1993), Saurugger and Woll (2008) and Woll (2006, 2008).
2   There are many books marketed to aspiring lobbyists. Probably the most intellectually meaningful is van Schendelen (2002).

6

MEMBER STATES

Lobbies, then, can influence debates and speak with Commission officials. They can push some issues up the agenda and perhaps cast doubt on the importance of others. When there is legislation – remembering again that legislation has not been the major form of EU health policy – they can try to influence MEPs. They can work with their member state equivalents or member organizations to influence states.

But in the end they do not decide. The biggest stakeholders in health systems are the member states themselves – the welfare states, quite literally. Not only are they powerful actors with direct votes, but also their structures and traditions shape the effectiveness and engagement of the interest groups from their health systems. Even if they cannot ensure that EU policy will reflect the preferences of their domestic health policy communities, they can at least find ways to alter legislation and ward off the worst potential problems (Jordan and Liefferink 2004: 234).

DIPLOMATIC, DEPARTMENTAL AND DELIBERATIVE

The structure of EU health decision-making means that co-ordination and activity must take place at multiple levels. This is naturally a challenge for member states.[1] There are, broadly, three forms of activity, each with different norms and stakes. They run from the diplomatic level, where politicians, diplomats and EU specialists engage in the serious matter of deciding how a member state shall vote in Council, through the under-studied departmental level at which most member states do most of their business, to the deliberative level at which lobbying and arguments shape agendas and policies – a place where member states can be wholly absent and lobbyists dominant.

Diplomatic

In diplomatic settings, the member state is speaking; votes and statements have force because they can bind member states. In the case of EU health policy, this means the Council of Ministers and the European Council (as well as the Intergovernmental Conferences that revise treaties).

The style of interaction comes about, fundamentally, because they are set up for the highest salience, tensest negotiations; this is the arena in which member states equip themselves to support their heads of state or leading ministers in tough negotiations and complex package deals. Policy is of less importance than process because procedural mistakes can be disastrous at this level. These arenas have diplomatic styles of interaction, first, because they are where the EU acts most like an international organization, second, because it is in the Council that member states vote as if they were individual people, and third, because that is where foreign ministries and EU co-ordinating units focus their attention. It is the exigencies of diplomacy that spawn implausible practices such as writing 'non-papers', which are draft proposals circulated by a government that do not have the status of formal proposals or papers laid before the body. They are emblematic of the careful, centralized style of this level of politics.

Diplomatic-level work dominates academic analysis of how states engage with the EU, just as much as it dominates the biographies of top politicians (it is not just the priorities of political journalists that make actual policy decisions vanish from so many accounts of political careers and EU summits). But, while important, it is only a smallish amount of all the work done in and on the EU, and its rules are distinct. That is why analyses of EU co-ordination that focus only on this world are slightly unreal: they capture the day-to-day activities of only a few people, and forget the many officials who engage constantly on the EU level and build networks that make formal arrangements a backstop. When the issue becomes less important and technical and removed from the Council (e.g. 1408/71 revisions), it becomes less co-ordinated, less diplomatic and more like the dominant level of EU health policymaking – the departmental level.

Departmental

The diplomatic level comes into play only when there is legislation or a treaty revision, and those are by no means the bulk of the activity in EU health policy (consider how little legislation matters in some of the areas discussed in Chapter 3). So while discussions of the diplomatic level dominate books on the co-ordination of EU policy, the diplomatic level is only a small part of what matters. Instead, much of the activity of EU health policy, such as participation in the various forums and committees, or discussions about Commission plans, is the responsibility of member state health ministries. They are the ones that send representatives to the meetings, and are charged in most member states with making policy, often with little oversight. They are the bureaucracies that produce policy – the policy bureaucracies (Page and Jenkins 2005).

The main reason is that these are highly technical areas that require expertise. Thinking through the interaction between zoonoses (animal-borne diseases) and human public health, or establishing safe blood supplies, requires a range of expertise that is found in and around health and agriculture ministries rather than generalist EU co-ordinators. Secondarily, they are low salience. Some can become high profile, but at those times more powerful actors than the health ministry can still become involved and change the direction of policy.

In summary, the departmental level comprises all of the formal EU forums that involve member state participation but which have not come to the attention of the EU co-ordinators and generalists of the diplomatic level. In this area, health and social security departments can have room to manoeuvre. It is also at this level where we see much more divergence how hard states try to co-ordinate, formulate a single position across departments, and genuinely pursue it. Some member states such as the UK are quite active at this level. Some have never been known to say anything.

Deliberative

The diplomatic and departmental levels of EU engagement make up the range of occasions on which a member state must be at the table. But there is a third level of EU activity, at which co-ordination is very difficult but there is tremendous variation in activity. This is the 'deliberative' level of policy – the background in which policy ideas are debated, items slip onto agendas, problems emerge, and

particular debates and issues receive their framings. Its manifest-
ations are all the things we study under the title of 'lobbying': attending events, developing networks, sharing information and in general
attempting to influence the course of debate. Member states lobby
each other (and work with central co-ordinators and their embassies
if need be), but more often they transmit information and argument
through networks of officials. Failure to engage at this level – i.e. an
overreliance on formal channels – is a sign of naivety (Sairinen and
Lindholm 2004).This level is also more 'democratic' than the
departmental and diplomatic levels; at this level, small states can be
as persuasive as big ones and member states are not much better
than lobbyists or regional governments.

WHAT MEMBER STATES DO

As Chapter 4 argued, the best adapted member states would be well
informed, tightly co-ordinated, nimble and highly active across all
three levels of policy. Of course, no member state is perfectly
adapted. No organization is simply a mirror of its environment, and
member states have more important things to mirror than the EU.
Co-ordination in public administration is an interesting topic, but it
is an error to think it is always a technical problem or one that is
always amenable to technical intervention (Page 2005). Failure to co-
ordinate is often political, and reflects a genuine divergence of opinion between politicians with genuine mandates. As a result, systems
that routinely fail to co-ordinate at the bureaucratic level can be that
way because their political systems do not encourage a good level of
co-ordination. These might not be functional bureaucratic structures, but they reflect important facts about the way those political
systems work.[2]

Identifying the differences can take some work. Most if not all
member states sound very similar on paper, with formal mechanisms
to determine who does what and how to produce opinions on EU
policy. Furthermore, their officials are all at least somewhat versed in
basic arts of politics: identifying key issues, sounding out important
players ahead of time, getting ministerial support lined up and
developing trust. So they are able to point out in interviews that the
formal procedure is clunkier and less important than the informal
work that it underpins. As a result, every member state sounds
superficially the same – reasonably competent and organized.

But that is like evaluating the decision-making of legislators by their ability to master the physical process of voting. Their political calculations and psychology are far more interesting than the act of pressing a button or holding up a hand, and likewise member states' decision-making styles in EU politics are more interesting and important than their basic ability to have opinions, sensible or not, by the time the Council working parties meet. For a start, not all opinions are sensible. As of October 2008, it was clear that at least four member states' stances in working parties on the proposed Patient Mobility Directive were not sensible: they denied the applicability of ECJ decisions on patient mobility. As one official from a different member state mildly noted, 'This means discussions tend to go around in circles'. What explains such phenomena as big, powerful, member states that ignore the previous ten years of treaty-based ECJ decisions?

Five basic factors explain how countries develop their different ways of participating in EU politics. They are the health systems, which influence both the stakes and the stakeholders; their constitutions, which constrain their options and decide who matters; their public administrations, which have their own habits; their models of EU policymaking, which were developed to deal with areas longer 'Europeanized' such as agriculture; and their health ministries, which are crucial actors but are mostly slow to emerge from their focus inward on health systems to a more European set of issues.

Health systems

The first, and probably least important contributor to a state's model of EU relations, is its health system. In part it matters because each health system has its own specific interaction with the EU. Health systems are extremely complex and finely balanced, with unexpected vulnerabilities. They are like old houses that have had many additions and repairs; removing a single door frame or prop can cause an unexpected collapse. This means that the differences in systems explain the particular challenges that they see in the EU, and their timing (for example, it was easier for national health services such as Spain and the UK to ignore the first patient mobility decisions because they were not social insurance countries; the French and Germans initially thought they were exempt because they used services in kind rather than reimbursements, but rapidly learned that the ECJ disagreed) (Gobrecht 1999).

What matters most is the way it shapes the political actors with an interest in health policy. The main axis on which they vary is the extent to which the leaders of the health system feel themselves tied into the state. In Germany, the social insurance funds (especially) take their 'self-administration' (*selbstverwaltung*) seriously and have the resources to develop their own EU lobbying activities. In Spain and France, by contrast, most actors in the health care system rely on the member state, or perhaps the more vigorous Spanish regional governments, to represent them and their interests. The health system therefore influences both the stakes for member states – what they are defending or need – and, via their traditions of interest intermediation, their performance at the departmental and deliberative levels.

Constitutions

Running a good health care system might play a role in a model of EU policy engagement, but compliance with a country's constitution matters more. This is partly because constitutions are fundamental laws. This means, for example, that German federal states participate in EU health policy because Germany's constitution obliges the federal government to take the interests of the federal states into account when participating in the EU.

Constitutions also matter because they reflect realities about the country. French formal centralization, Spanish fragmentation and the German combination of interpenetration and fragmentation all reflect profound political and social realities of their countries. Their constitutions perpetuate them, true enough, but they also reflect them, and even a new constitution would not make Germany or Spain into a hierarchical state like France. This is the basis of the profound pattern visible in most policy areas that regional governments' power in EU affairs is directly predicted by their power in the member state.

Public administrations

A state's public administration is partly a reflection of the tensions and priorities right now. But it is also a reflection of many other decisions and developments that have a life, and an influence, of their own. A member state's EU policymaking will reflect its model of public administration, its standard operating procedures and its culture. The past is not history; it is not even past. It lives on in bureaucracies that bear the imprint of generations of political reform.

The most important variations in public administration in this study lie on a small number of axes. The most important one is the role of the tenured civil service relative to political appointees. There is a tenured, professional civil service with lifetime employment in all four of the states here. What varies is its role at the top – the extent to which members are present and making major decisions at the top. The UK, with its Whitehall model, still has non-partisan civil servants acting at high levels (and many of its special advisers are focused on media rather than policy). Germany has more political appointees, but career civil servants still bear most of the burden of making decisions with politicians. France has a determined political level – the ministerial *cabinet* – that can override the more technical civil servants. Spain has a similar political level of ministerial advisers, but also has a long tradition of political appointees at many rungs of the civil service and interpenetration with academia. In practice, this means that each public administration has a distinctive combination of generalism, expertise, attitude to lobbies and engagement with the EU (Liefferink and Jordan 2004).

The other important axis, which often has its roots in constitutional principles and history but which takes on a life of its own, is the extent of departmental autonomy and distinctiveness. This is a key issue for co-ordination because departments can, de facto or de jure, be highly autonomous and culturally distinct in some systems (such as the German). This can reduce the effectiveness of the central co-ordinators at the diplomatic level of engagement, and can also allow departments great scope to make their own policy in their areas of interest. Finally, culture matters in itself. Organizations have their established ways of doing things, and shared values revealed in practice, and that shapes what they will do.

Models of EU policymaking

Constitutions and public administration come together with the exigencies of EU politics to produce each state's model for EU relations. The EU model in most cases reflects its history, and especially decisions taken around the time that the member state joined the EU. Since then, however, it has been extensively worked out in departments beyond health. It often includes formal or informal EU career paths, and even some careers focused on EU health issues (in our cases, they exist in France, Germany and the UK). Given that politicians, central co-ordinators and other line departments all understand the model, it is no surprise that they typically extend it to health.

At the diplomatic level, there is a great deal of convergence between member states (Wessels et al. 2003b). Every member state has a Permanent Representation because Council procedure requires it. But while the vessels remain similar, the contents differ. Every member state has a dedicated unit and minister to deal with European affairs, usually housed in some combination of the foreign affairs, economics/finance, and central (prime ministerial) departments. In many states that Europe minister's real status and networks varies substantially over time. These are all relatively logical outgrowths of EU rules and the cautious, generalist, nature of diplomatic-level activity. How they work in practice, at the departmental, diplomatic and deliberative levels, is a very different matter. Each member state applies its template for EU affairs to health, but it can produce unexpected effects in combination with other issues, such as the final variable, the make-up of the health ministry itself.

Health ministries

The central actors in this book are the health ministries themselves of each member state.[3] The importance of the departmental level of politics in the EU, and the autonomy of departments at that stage, make them the central actors. It is in the health ministries, and in their international units, that the member state has the best chance of influencing policy and agenda in the deliberative and departmental levels – in other words at the crucial formative stages that shape the policy.

Health ministries are understudied and bear some heavy political burdens already, above and beyond the complex task of managing health care (Ettelt et al. 2008). Much prescriptive health policy literature says that health ministries should be more powerful. That would allow them not only to run health services but also to shape broader policy in ways that improve overall health and fight off cuts to the welfare state (Dawson and Morris 2008; Rico Gómez et al. 2007; Yach 2005). That is a poor fit with their usual weakness. Ministries and their ministers are strong if they command money (a large budget), law (the ability to make regulations or shepherd legislation) or resources (technical expertise and infrastructure) (Rose 1987). By that standard, most health ministries score poorly. In Spain, for example, the health ministry in Madrid has none because regional governments control all three. In Germany, the federal health ministry makes laws, but most of the money and resources are in the hands of the social partners. Worse, the development of EU policy threatens exactly the reverse of empowerment for all health ministries: a reduction in the importance of health ministries on the grounds that they are less engaged with relevant EU policies than economics, finance or even social security ministries that have been working with the EU on competition, state aids, public procurement or the internal market.

So even if we do not ask health ministries to expand the role of health in policy, we must at least rely on them to fight off prospective reductions in the importance of health and in the autonomy of health policymaking. Part of the problem is a structural one. The health ministers' Council is a weak subformation of the Employment and Social Policy Council. It rarely gets to discuss issues of the most importance for health systems (especially various internal market laws). If health ministries are to defend (let alone expand) their role in policymaking they must learn about and intervene in other ministries' business and do so at the EU level.

In one of our countries, the UK, the health ministry (Department of Health – DH), is relatively powerful. That is because it directly runs England's National Health Service, with its 1 million employees and enormous budget, and because the Westminster system means that a UK government can change the NHS with far less political resistance than in the other three states (Greer 2005; Hacker 2004). It is also because health is a far higher profile issue in politics in the UK than in the other states. France, Germany and Spain each enjoy a basic level of popular and elite satisfaction with the basic structure of their health care systems, and there has been far less political pressure than in the UK (where one interviewee noted that 'one of our ministers is on the *Today* programme almost every day').[4] It is important to remember, contextually, that health policy in the UK is constant front-page news whereas it is something of a backwater in the other three states.

If they are even to understand the challenges that they face, they face an internal challenge. Health departments tend to turn inward, to focus on their systems. They are the masters of the secret garden of health policy. But this is a risk because parochialism is a risk. A discussion of environmental policy in the UK sums up the potential future fate of health in all four countries:

Parochial in its outlook . . . the [Department of Environment] failed to engage positively in the early, critical, phases of EU environmental policy development. . . . The [department] also sanctioned many important EU policies in the mistaken belief that they would not unduly disrupt British environmental policy. But when these policies were eventually implemented in Britain, they were transmogrified in ways that surprised many Whitehall departments. . . . The result was Europeanization on the EU's terms, rather than Whitehall's.

(Jordan 2002: xvii)

The extent to which health departments culturally adapt to Europe (Jordan 2003) will decide whether they share the fate of the UK's environment ministry. In other words, health departments generally lack what one interviewee called a 'European culture'. Health and EU policy are still a rare combination of skills. Such a culture would make them effective actors. And once the EU becomes so important that they must adapt, the scope for influence will be much less than it is now. Europeanization that way would not be on their terms.

PROBLEMS THAT STATES FACE

The basic issue for states is simple: how can they influence EU policy in a way that maintains the integrity and autonomy of their health systems (and, in the best of circumstances, promotes health and solidarity)? This means that they must ask how to balance different priorities – the integrity of their constitution against their effectiveness in the EU, or the political rewards of a ministerial focus on health services versus the boring but important work of EU influence. They have a very limited ability to decide this balance for themselves. Everything from the constitutional status of regional government to organizational culture and different health systems shapes what they imagine and do. But we can identify the problems that face them in trying to be effective agents for health in EU policymaking.

Energy and culture

Participation in EU meetings can also be very boring; many of them start with a *tour de table* at which all 27 member states read out their positions. Active, dynamic ministers – who might otherwise be the most effective – are quite sensibly reluctant to sit through this and other European rituals. But sitting through them and thereby showing respect is the way to start to use the process; politicians and officials who shun them, or who propose some sort of reduced directorate of big states, typically alienate the excluded states and achieve little. Consider one experienced official's comment:

Lots of the work is uninteresting. An experience at a Council meeting – Luxembourg 2000, for example. The same day there was a meeting of the justice and internal affairs [Council]. The chair, the Luxembourg health minister, invited all the ministers to a working lunch. [German federal minister] Seehofer said, 'I am not going to stay and listen to this rubbish. I am going to go' – and he went. The Luxembourg chair gave the word to [minister Bernard] Kouchner from France. He spoke – half an hour, open, fantastic. Then the other ministers spoke, all using prepared statements. And *three* Austrian ministers spoke, and all read their papers aloud. The [other] German minister said, 'Do I have to stay for this?' We [officials] said no, and he left. So [an official] represented Germany and it was the only country not to speak! [The official] said Germany doesn't have to say anything because everything has been said. An unstructured meeting for 50 ministers. It was ridiculous . . .

This unusual and, for most people, unpleasant experience creates a problem for states, especially the international divisions of health ministries charged with EU health issues. They always face a challenge in getting political and expert attention to EU health issues.[5] When there are interesting issues, they often involve co-opting experts onto European committees, which creates a new problem because committees of like-minded experts can often create political spillover; by meeting on an EU level to discuss issues, they can create pressures for new EU competencies as a result of their work on the committees. Such an expansion of EU competencies and independent experts of networks are not a priority for most member states.

The problem of gaining high-level attention is exacerbated by the nature of EU health politics now. They are low-profile and vague and discussions can seem alarmist precisely because the basic framework of EU health policy is not yet set. But that is precisely why activity now is likely to be more effective than activity in the future. Marginal changes later will take far more effort than fundamental changes of direction now.

Poor co-ordination

You need to get in and sell a line six months before the proposal is even published. Some member states can't make their decisions

fast enough . . . or somebody in the capital comes in late and
changes the decision.

(UK official, October 2008)

Poor co-ordination has all the flaws noted in a wealth of literature
(Wright 1996): it reduces effectiveness because it means that states
cannot focus their energies on their priorities; cannot make package
deals; cannot equip their officials with the best and most complete
dossiers; cannot reduce their ability to trip over themselves; cannot
pledge their regional governments or assist them; and cannot, in
extremis, keep different departments from doing contradictory
things in Council. That makes it a reasonable enemy of most reflect-
ive practitioners. It is also unusual, and perhaps bad manners, to
disparage co-ordination.

One form of co-ordination that is not always noted is between
generalists and specialists. EU specialists are often concerned about
preserving subsidiarity (restricting EU activity), promoting overall
government strategies (which can require trading off health) and
focusing attention on areas dictated by a larger strategy. Line department officials, such as those in health ministries, are often more
interested by substantive policy objectives (Geuijen et al. 2007). It is
analogous to the division that exists in federal states, found in ministries such as the Spanish Ministry of Public Administrations (MAP)
or the Canadian federal Minister of Intergovernmental Affairs. Officials from those units are focused on the constitutional division of
resources and responsibilities and often exist in tension with line
officials who want to make substantive policy. In the same way, EU
generalists focused on preserving subsidiarity or even trading off
health in favour of a greater priority sometimes exist in tension with
line officials who are interested in making substantive policy and
using new EU networks or opportunities. The latter are very likely to
pursue substantive aims without much regard to subsidiarity or
treaty bases.

Good co-ordination

But co-ordination is not always a good thing. Co-ordination simply
means that a member state determines a priority and organizes itself
to pursue that priority. This is obviously much more satisfactory for
those who support the priority. In tobacco regulation, for example,
there is often a cleavage in member states between the economics and
finance ministries, which rely on tobacco taxes for revenue and are

often sympathetic to such businesses, and health ministries, which are usually more interested in reducing the public health problems created by tobacco use. In many states the reverse holds with pharmaceuticals: health ministries can be very closely connected to pharmaceutical companies, to the irritation of finance ministries that are aware of the costs of new drugs; this criticism was loudest in my Spanish interviews but appeared in all four.[6] As a rule of thumb, finance and economics ministers, and ministries, are more powerful than health ministries. If the internal priority-setting mechanism in a given state means that the health ministry's support for anti-tobacco policy is overridden by the finance ministry, then co-ordination has produced a bad outcome from the point of view of public health. Even if that does not happen, the ability to make big package deals can damage weaker departments. Spain's priorities include border co-operation, fisheries, regional aid and agriculture, and not health. When it trades off less important issues, it can trade off health.

The point is that information is a weapon. Poor co-ordination can be rational and desirable if co-ordination would produce an unsatisfactory policy outcome (Jordan and Schout 2006: 164–165). In our member states, we see the logic most clearly in Germany, where there is a strong tradition of ministerial autonomy and where the health ministry is far down the scale of ministerial power. In Germany, the health ministry will often find that it is more rational to 'hide', letting policies on health issues develop their own momentum in Brussels. That way, when they do come to the attention of the finance and economics ministry, they will be more likely to survive its opposition. This is rational from the point of view of the health ministry, and probably of the health of Europeans, but it would fall victim to improved interministerial co-ordination.

Constitutional change by the back door

Constitutions are not just an interesting part of the explanation for why states act as they do. They are also a value in themselves. A constitution, at least in theory, is the ultimate expression of how a people wishes to govern itself. It allocates authority and balances between territorial, political and social interests in distinctive ways, and no country changes its constitution lightly. In so far as that is the case, there should be a strong presumption against changing constitutions through any mechanism other than their own amending procedures.

The constitutional problem is simple: the European Union changes constitutional divisions of power, concentrating it in central executives. It speeds the decline of parliamentary power, but only marginally; while member states' engagement in the EU is dominated by executives, so is policymaking in most member states. Parliamentary oversight committees of various sorts are weak for the same reason that most parliamentary oversight committees are weak in domestic politics: party discipline. There never was a golden age of legislative autonomy and declines in the power of legislatures can rarely be attributed to the EU (Raunio and Hix 2000). There is not enough change, or enough of a role, to discuss them further.

A more important problem, for the member states that have powerful regional governments, is that it alters their internal allocation of authority. If a member state's constitutional law gives its regional governments responsibility for health without much restriction (as with the Basque Country or Scotland), then the development of EU policies is bad news for the region's autonomy.[7]

First, it subjects their policymaking to new, EU restrictions. This has *substantive* effects, limiting their autonomy and possible options. Second, the member states are far more important in EU politics than the regional governments. Europeanization of health reduces their influence over the *policymaking* at the same time that it reduces their autonomy. The Council is a key legislative body while the Committee of the Regions scarcely bears noticing. If regional governments do not have input into EU policy, they see their influence over their health policies removed to the EU and member states. Regions are major actors in health; in the UK and Spain health is usually their biggest single power and they dominate it. Losing control over not only health policy but also health policymaking to a Brussels world where they are just lobbyists is unpalatable, not just to autonomist regional politicians but to anybody who believes that the German, Spanish and UK constitutions reflect profound and democratically legitimate values.

Regions experimented during the 1990s with a variety of ways to defend their autonomy and substantive interests in the EU, ranging from lobbying offices in Brussels to the Committee of the Regions to the right to represent their member states in Council (and in some cases, such as Germany in education councils, effectively freeze out their federal government). Almost two decades of collective experimentation by regions across Europe has taught some uncomfortable lessons (Jeffery 2005; Jeffery and Palmer 2007). The most effective thing to be, for influencing EU institutions, is a member state. Power over the member state, being 'built into' policymaking, is far more effective than lobbying or participation in the Committee of the Regions. Even if regions have been poor health lobbyists, with limited resources and small-scale preoccupations, their responsibility for health systems should make them major actors. They should be major lobbyists because they run many of the health systems that the EU institutions purport to regulate. But being political actors above and beyond being lobbyists means gaining influence over their member states. That is ideologically difficult for many regional leaders, especially some from nationalist parties faced with uncooperative central states. But this is a topic full of paradoxes. The best way to preserve regional autonomy in the face of a Europe that reduces it is to enhance regional power over the member state.

CONCLUSION

The question is: how do we prioritise what people do to ensure inputting and influencing the right ways. Rather than ad hoc, with people going to meetings because they are interested as a personal project on the side.

(UK official, March 2006)

The perfectly adapted EU member state would be sure of itself, informed, co-ordinated, nimble and active. But that perfect state could exist only in a very different world. States cannot, should not and do not reorganize themselves to influence the EU (Page 2003). They have responsibilities, above all to their own constitutions and the voters whose values they supposedly embody. That means, for example, avoiding constitutional change by stealth. EU health policy redistributes power over health away from a variety of regional governments. Like most EU health policy, it does so without any democratic legitimacy (let alone the high barriers of referenda that would be required for any other effort to so restrict the autonomy of a Catalonia or Wales). States are also constrained by the inherited cultures and rules of their bureaucracies, especially health ministries that could dominate the park if they ceased to act in ways better adapted to the days of the secret garden.

It is too simple to say that this is simply a question of co-ordination. Co-ordination, despite its immense intellectual and practical appeal, is not always as desirable as it may seem. If the policy goal for health policy is to create policies and a policymaking structure that defend the autonomy of health policymakers in member states (regional or state) and even to shift EU policies in favour of health, then co-ordination might just snuff out their priorities in the face of others. Chapters 7–10 discuss the ways in which the health systems, constitutions, public administrations, EU models and health ministries of France, Germany, the UK and Spain explain their approach to EU health policy, including the extent to which they suffer from or overcome problems of energy, co-ordination and constitutional change.

NOTES

1   The main texts on the subject, with reviews of older treatments, are Bursens (2007), Kassim et al. (2000, 2001), Laffan (2007), Wallace (2005) and Wessels et al. (2003a).
2   Size of country is one variable I do not discuss; smaller countries tend to focus more, need not always put so much effort into co-ordination, and do not have the resources to cover every dossier (see Kassim et al. 2000, 2001). But in our four countries, resources are less of a constraint than the other priorities that these big bureaucracies must balance, and I do not discuss size further. Like most EU member states, France, Germany, Spain and the UK can afford a few dedicated civil servants for EU affairs.
3   This was not what I initially expected, given that the literature on co-ordination focuses overwhelmingly what happens at the diplomatic level, and most literature on actual EU policymaking pays little systematic attention to just who speaks for a given member state at a given time.
4   The *Today* programme is a highly influential morning radio show on the BBC that often sets the media agenda for the next 24 hours and is known for grilling ministers just after 8 a.m.
5   I attended one event in April 2005 that brought together more than 30 EU health policy experts in an attempt to convey the importance of the EU to a leading health department official. To increase the chances that he would attend and listen, it was held over an excellent dinner in a prestigious central address and the organizers informally told each of us 'not to bore him'.
6   Of course, a multi-year lobbying offensive by the pharmaceutical industry has brought DG Enterprise and a number of finance ministries to support them with the argument the pharmaceuticals are a major EU growth industry. This might reduce pressure on costs of medicines.
7   This means that the giant 1990s debate about a potential 'Europe of the regions' was misguided. For longer discussions of how European integration could *reduce* regional power and autonomy, and the reasons

why regions' most effective strategy often is to work with and through member states, see Goldsmith (2003), Greer (2009b), Hooghe and Marks (2001), Jeffery (2005), Jeffery and Palmer (2007) and Tarrow (2004).

7

FRANCE

With François Briatte

France shares a paradox with the UK: its highly unified state and political culture has a tradition of independent action that often takes badly to European constraint, but that same highly unified state and political culture underpin an effective model of engagement in EU health policymaking. It is no surprise that both member states are regularly accused of hypocrisy. It is virtually written into their constitutions.

SYSTEM AND STAKES

France is an 'excellent ideal type . . . as an example [of] clashes of "state-centric" national political systems with the pluralistic multi-level system that is the European Union' (Szukala 2003: 216). French concern with the integrity and sovereignty of its state, runs the argument, make the extension of European competencies in itself something of a problem for many French policymakers. Expanding EU competencies reveal the basic tension between Europe as a strategy for French projection and Europe as a threat to French nationality (Sauger 2008).

Of course, that picture is a bit too neat. France is changing, as many books have argued, with debate often focused on whether France is becoming less state-centric and nationalist, or whether the old pictures were overdrawn (Kassim 2008; A. Smith 2006). But relative to the other member states in this study, France is certainly distinctive for its generally diplomatic approach to EU policies, its centralization and its effectiveness.

System

Health care in France is administered through a statutory health insurance model, mainly financed through payroll contributions and regulated through negotiations between sickness funds, representatives of the medical professions and the state. About 85 per cent of the population belongs to a single large insurance fund, the Caisse Nationale d'Assurance Maladie des Travailleurs Salariés (CNAMTS), placed under close state supervision. This specific institutional arrangement reflects a long history of compromise between the demand for universal coverage and specific claims from mutual aid societies that predated the demand for universal coverage in the post-war context (Dutton 2007; Palier 2005). Recent reforms have accentuated the state-controlled character of the French health system by creating a national union of sickness funds directed by a higher civil servant appointed by the government (Franc and Polton 2004). There is also an increasing element of tax finance and universality in the French system, since the CNAMTS now provides means-tested basic and complementary coverage to the poorest part of the population on the basis of residence (Hassenteufel and Palier 2005). The result is that power in the French health care system, as in many other aspects of French public administration, tends to stick to the centre, and local actors put a great deal of effort into finding ways to influence the decision-makers at the centre.

The social insurance nature of the system, and the concomitant freedoms of providers, are also the basis of most of the problems France might face in health care. Patients' free choice of doctor is an essential aspect of health care which recent gatekeeping schemes have made more costly in some circumstances, yet left intact in principle. The private sector plays a crucial role in health care supply, as most ambulatory and specialist care is delivered by liberal practitioners, whereas hospital care is also delivered by publicly owned and privately owned entities. Traditionally, the Ministry of Health regulates and provides some capital and core funding to the hospitals while the sickness funds reimburse doctors and treatments directly.

Stakes

This system is obviously vulnerable to competition law, state aids and public procurement challenges. A set of legal and associational rules constrains what providers can do and operate while there are variety of public sector subsidies to hospitals that make them competitive and cross-subsidize the less profitable or more costly services. Working out how to maintain solidarity – risk-pooling – under anything like EU public procurement rules is a major headache for French policymakers. Patient choice of provider combined with local subsidies to the municipal hospital might make for a satisfactory health system, but it is basically open to the risk that alternative providers will try to open the market and challenge the subsidies or limits on medical entrepreneurship. Likewise, the French reliance on supplementary health insurance for co-payment means that an important part of its health care system is subject to EU regulation of private insurance (Thomson and Mossialos 2009).

France is less vulnerable to the problems of patient mobility (formally, since the *Vanbraekel* case), although it has had to pay compliance costs because the simple French system of reimbursing providers does not translate easily across borders (for adaptation to date, see Inspection générale des affaires sociales 2006b: 335–388). In the areas with a high degree of patient mobility – and every one of France's land frontiers has a noticeable amount of it – there is a tradition of agreements governing cross-border mobility (Harant 2006). Some of them date back decades, and many are overlaid with high-profile 'Euroregions' that receive EU funding and publicity for their ability to surmount borders. French policymakers – and their German counterparts – thought these relationships were stable, technical and not very interesting (relationships across the Pyrenees are interesting, and sometimes frustrating, but that is because of intergovernmental problems on the Spanish side).

To what extent is the French constitution open to backdoor change? Probably not much. That is because so much power in health care is still in the hands of the central state. The problem for France and many of the French, however, is precisely the fit of EU politics with its traditional, 'unitary' political culture, which is very state-centric and emphasizes access to and the use of state power (Grossman and Sauger 2008; A. Smith 2006). This means that Europeanization might feel more traumatic and produce more transformative effects on policymaking than in other countries that are more used to consensus and less accustomed to decisive action. That feeds into a much noted characteristic of French politics: France is a country where autonomy in itself is a particular value. French policymakers often deny the influence of even less coercive forms of Europeanization such as the Open Method of Co-ordination, although they can become strategic resources in domestic policymaking (Palier and Petrescu 2007: 67–69). French policymakers do not have a basic cultural conviction that they should learn from Europe; they prefer to think of France as a European policymaker that influences the EU and other states, rather than as a policy-taker (Ehrel et al. 2005; Risse 2001: 228). The stellar performance of the French health system in international comparisons such as the WHO *World Health Report 2000* has led many stakeholders to conclude that there is no reason to get advice from their EU partners or the Commission.

EXPLAINING FRANCE'S EU HEALTH POLICY

French engagement with the EU puts the emphasis on the effectiveness of the French state, not only putting considerable effort into co-ordination across ministries but also engaging in a heroic effort to co-ordinate and lead, or at least follow, all the various networks, interests and lobbyists from France who engage with the EU. (For a classic discussion, see Lequesne 1993.) In a complex environment such as the EU, with so many ways to fragment member state governments and draw out professional and social networks independent of governments, this might be enormously effective. While it will be ultimately futile, because both France and the EU are too complicated, the effort has contributed to French power within health policy and fits squarely in a long French unitary tradition.

Constitution

The French constitution is famously centralized and the French state one of the most famous characters in the whole literature of politics. Believable, if apocryphal, stories abound of French education ministers knowing exactly what each 11-year-old child in the country would be reading at a given time. French centralization is easy to overstate, but in EU health policy France is centralized. Characterizing responsibility at the top can also be problematic in France's semi-presidential system, due to the possibility of 'cohabitation' in which the President and the Prime Minister come from different parties. The dual executive model was essentially premised on a level of unified control that it did not create – it gives the Prime Minister (head of government, responsible to the legislature) a different base than the President (head of state, elected through a two-round majoritarian system). The relationship between the President and the Prime Minister, who share executive power, is prone to instability when Prime Minister and President are rivals or even of different parties (Bell 2000). France went through three periods of such 'cohabitation' between 1986 and 2002 (1986–1988, 1993–1995 and 1997–2002) but after changing election sequencing (so that parliaments are elected a month after the President) it reverted to presidential superiority (Levy and Skatch 2008). The President can lead cabinet meetings and therefore make forays into governmental policy even if he or she does not control the machinery of ministerial power or the legislative majority; the result can be conflict with the Prime Minister.

Public administration

French public administration is a distinct and enormously influential approach in its own right, one that is little understood by those bred in other traditions but which influence shapes the operations of many states including almost the whole Mediterranean world. Its combination of hierarchy, a powerful state, elite self-preservation through networking, rules as the legitimacy of all activity, and democratic party politics create a state structure that can perplex outside observers. It includes a variety of seemingly contradictory elements: a powerful bureaucracy and a high degree of political influence and appointment; a small elite with a high degree of closure but also a high degree of fragmentation; distinct political and bureaucratic worlds but with considerable traffic across their border (Chevallier 1997); bureaucratic *corps* united by education that stretch across politics and business such as the elite *énarques* (graduates of the *Ecole Nationale d'Administration*); fierce party politics combined with very long careers that span many changes of government (Rouban 1999); firm rules, and their flexible interpretation. The *énarques* must coexist with the pharmacist from *Madame Bovary*.

The pattern that emerges from the reconciliation of these contradictions is that France has a very clearly delimited technical level of officials in the ministry. Most of the officials in the ministry who deal with the EU operate on this level. Their role is firmly subordinate, however, to the political level, which includes the ministerial *cabinet* as well as some of the most politically engaged officials at the top. The key group of officials, whose careers tend to land on the political side of the line, are members of a bureaucratic body chosen by education. These *corps* appear throughout French public administration; the *corps* in health is the Inspectorate-General of Social Affairs (IGAS) as well as former members from the 'social chamber' of the *Cour des comptes* (Genieys and Smyrl 2008).

Ministerial decision-making usually passes through specific *cabinet* members as well as through the minister, who are likely to be decisive policy players. *Cabinet* members are often young and from a variety of elite political and bureaucratic backgrounds. They can draw on the department but also have to develop wider networks through French politics, reflecting their position as political generalists rather than technical experts.

The other well-documented, much-lamented, generally overblown and endlessly confused problem in France is the relative weakness of civil society relative to the state (Rosanvallon 2004). If French domestic politics encourages interests to develop influence within central bureaucracies in Paris, they might not develop the habit of investing in autonomous lobbyists. Instead, there is a tendency for French interests of all sorts to invest in relationships, formal or informal, with the state (Keeler and Hall 2001) and French public authorities to be suspicious of professional lobbyists (Grossman 2005). This is not necessarily a bad thing because it is not at all clear why one would want professional lobbyists. It is just that they are an undeniably important feature of the EU, and that means that a reluctance to lobby means overreliance on the French state. The lack of French lobbying appears to be particularly striking in health; the IGAS, doctors and other dominant players in the French health system are slow to engage with the EU as lobbyists.

Health ministry

The very success of the French health care system – which scores well on most indicators and is seen as satisfactory at elite and public levels – is part the reason that the health ministry is weak. Within the state, the fragmented organization of public health services, also a historical constant in France (Ménard 2006) and fierce competition between agencies means that ministerial capacity over health issues is shared by several structures, among which 'the Ministry of Health is not the sole player, and sometimes not even the most prominent one' (Cour des Comptes 2004: 143).[1] Despite their heightened control over negotiations of medical fees, health care is not directly administered by state authorities. The ministry itself enjoys direct control over only a residual part of the total health care budget, since health providers are reimbursed by sickness funds directly. As a consequence, it has been constantly dwarfed by ministries with larger budgets, resources, and political visibility.

Minister of Health is a low-ranking post and the ministry's place in the bureaucratic structure of the French state is also low ranking. The Inspectorate-General of Social Affairs (IGAS), the relevant *corps* for the ministry, is low status as French bureaucratic *corps* go, and the National School of Public Health (ENSP) often thought to be the school for those whose test scores were not good enough to get them into the *Ecole Nationale d'Administration* (a perception as important than any truth). Furthermore, the ministry's implementation administration at the local level is staffed by public health inspection doctors who are held in low esteem by their clinician peers (Inspection générale des affaires sociales 2006a).

Fluctuating ministerial boundaries reflect this weakness; the Ministry of Health alternates between being paired with worthy issues that ordinarily do not receive enough attention (such as the needs of the disabled or voluntary sector activities) and being paired with social affairs. Social affairs is another area that the state does not always directly administer and that the bureaucratic elite perceive as a 'professional dead end' (Eymeri 2001; Genieys and Smyrl 2008) (see Table 7.1). Between 1997 and 2002, health was left to junior ministers who were subordinated to an overarching (and, under a left-wing government, prominent) Ministry of Employment and

Table 7.1 Ministerial headings and hierarchical rankings 1995–2007

Prime Minister	Main ministry	Rank	Junior ministry	Rank
A. Juppé (I), May 1995	Ministry of Public Health and Health Insurance (E. Hubert)	14/42		
A. Juppé (II), November 1995	Ministry of Labour and Social Affairs (J. Barrot)	6/32	Secretary of State for Health and Social Security (H. Gaymard)	32/32
L. Jospin 1997–2001	Ministry of Employment and Solidarity (M. Aubry, *then* E. Guigou)	1/26	Secretary of State for Health, *then* Secretary of State for Health and Social Action (B. Kouchner, *then* D. Gillot)	18/26

			Minister-Delegate for Health (B. Kouchner)		10/33
J.-P. Raffarin (I), 2002	Ministry of Health, Family and Disabled People (J.-F. Mattéi)	10/27			
J.-P. Raffarin (II), 2002	Ministry of Health, Family and Disabled People (J.-F. Mattéi)	10/38			
J.-P. Raffarin (III), 2004	Ministry of Health and Social Protection, *then* Ministry of Solidarities, Health and Family (P. Douste-Blazy)	8/43	Secretary of State for Health Insurance (X. Bertrand)		39/43
Dominique de Villepin 2005	Ministry of Health and Solidarities (X. Bertrand)	9/31	Ministry-Delegate for Social Security, Old People, Disabled People and Family (P. Bas)		27/31
François Fillon 2007	Ministry of Health, Youth and Sports (R. Bachelot-Narquin)	12/20			

Note: 'Rank' indicates the protocolary rank in the ministerial hierarchy.
Contrary to the British system, French secretaries of state hold a *minor* position in government (for example, they do not systematically attend governmental cabinet meetings).
Source: Briatte, F. (2006) *Lutter contre les inégalités de santé en France et en Grande-Bretagne*, IEP Grenoble, Grenoble.

Jacques Chirac did not include a health minister in his first government, in March 1986.

FRANCE'S EU MODEL IN HEALTH

The French model of centralized public administration combines with a very clear geopolitical stance that emphasizes the state's power, autonomy and international figure. Not only does the French approach to administration emphasize hierarchy and unity (even if it is latent), but also the French approach to international and

European affairs emphasizes the unity, co-ordination and effectiveness of the state. To a large extent, French policymakers tend to adopt a more 'diplomatic' approach, jealous of sovereignty, disinclined to view the EU as just another layer of lawmaking, and prone to act as a unified state on the European and world stage (Balme and Woll 2005; Drake 2005).

Diplomatic

This emphasis translates into one of Europe's most sophisticated and determined co-ordinating mechanisms at the diplomatic level. At the bottom are the officials of the Ministry of Health (and Solidarity). The international affairs unit of the ministry, the Délégation aux Affaires Européennes et Internationals, collects and organizes information about proposals, impact analyses and possible political issues as well as keeping a watch on implementation. But in keeping with the role of political, rather than civil service, appointees at the top, the ministerial *cabinet* engages with strategic, political issues and is able to draw on kinds of political power and connections that technical officials lack. So interministerial conflicts in the formulation of an EU line might get picked up at the technical level, but unless they are simple misunderstandings they are likely to be referred to the political level.

The next body in the chain linking the ministry to the EU is the Secretariat-General for European Affairs, the SGAE.[2] The SGAE is a central unit attached to the Prime Minister that is responsible for co-ordination, that is collecting information about all events that might influence France and determine French goals and strategies. However surprising it might be to those accustomed to the British and French administrative traditions, a powerful and relatively autonomous central co-ordinating agency such as the SGAE, with a serious claim to handle all EU policy, is the exception not the rule in Europe.

The SGAE predates the EU itself, but it was reorganized in 2005 (Lanceron 2007) in response to problems with implementation of EU law and the general discontent discussed in a report led by Admiral Lanxade (Commissariat général du Plan 2002) that described the situation as 'acceptable, but with more and more difficulties'. The report criticized France for many of the same things that other member states reproach themselves: problems of communication with Permanent Representation, badly organized priorities, bad use of experts and 'a deficit of strategy'. The subsequent changes did not fundamentally alter it; many of them simply increased clarity about what it actually did (including its new, and much more understandable name SGAE).

The SGAE does what most EU co-ordinating units aspire to do, that is co-ordinate between ministries, provide expertise on all aspects of the EU (including access to personal networks), transmit information and encourage strategy if not formulate it. It also has a role, more salient since 2005, in tracking the transposition of directives. That was in large part the motive for action; Lanxade's 'acceptable' situation might not have deserved change had it not been for embarrassment with the poor French transposition and implementation record, and the SGAE has a relatively large unit tracking implementation of EU legislation.

The SGAE is an elite administrative unit, made up mostly of officials on short-term secondment from across the different ministries (mostly finance and economics) who are gaining central experience as part of rapid career progression or who were unhappy in their home ministries (Lanceron 2007). It distributes papers about EU developments and hosts constant meetings at which ministries agree the French position on diplomatic-level questions; if no agreed position emerges, it will refer the question to political levels.

The specific arrangements that connect the SGAE, Prime Minister, President and various ministries including Foreign Affairs tend to change at the top with each President and Prime Minister. Analyses of diplomatic-level French EU policy tend to focus on the different configurations of President, Prime Minister and head of SGAE (whose title changes) (Hayward and Wright 2002; Lanceron 2007; Lequesne 1993). Paying attention to personalities and the political power of each individual is crucial in this kind of very elite analysis.

So far, cohabitation and tensions between Matignon (the Prime Minister) and the Elysée Palace (the President) have not spilled over directly into health. The main reason is that specific EU health issues have not received much attention from presidents. EU health policy might have begun with a 'Europe Against Cancer' initiative proposed by French President Mitterrand, but most health issues have not been sufficiently high profile to engage presidents. But even if the bureaucracy does not change much, the effect of changes in the President or Prime Minister 'changes everything', as one interviewee said. It does this because these are small units that are closely tied to top politicians, and so the autonomy and efficacy of co-ordinators and ministries is affected by the presence or absence of unpredictable countervailing, or even dominant, powers across the river in the Elysée Palace.

These problems do not normally affect the everyday flow of paper and work on ordinary EU law. The SGAE is the guardian of the French state's views and votes, and is good at co-ordinating and forcing meetings to resolve issues on which there is divergence; beyond that, it is able to co-ordinate a wide range of general policy stances. Finally, day-to-day co-ordination is ensured by the simple fact that the SGAE transmits all the formal papers (emails) to the Permanent Representation. Naturally this volume of email allows some issues to slip, but the SGAE takes its gatekeeping role seriously enough to prevent most nontrivial contradictions.

The French Permanent Representation in Brussels, then, provides the personnel who attend key meetings and handle the work of the diplomatic level. The health desk officer at the French Permanent Representation is seconded from the Ministry of Health. This increases the technical skill and connection with the ministry of the Permanent Representation, which in principle improves the connection of France with health debates at all levels. Like all Permanent Representations, its members pick up tactical and policy information that allows them to influence decisions in Paris. But their autonomy is relatively limited because Paris is more capable than most member states of formulating a *detailed* line and imposing it. Some EU representatives attend Councils with only vague (or sometimes no) orders. That is very rare in France. The machine does its job; there will be a *dossier* and a position and the Permanent Representation can focus on promoting it.

This diplomatic effectiveness, and tendency to view the EU as a creature of states with France as a leader, also affects the French response to EU legislation once it is passed. France is a habitual non-implementer. An extensive study found that there was serious variation between groups of countries in their approach to implementation; while a few Scandinavian countries were fast and faithful in implementation, most countries would use their margin to delay or alter directives in response to domestic political pressures. France was one of a small number of countries that would, essentially, ignore major EU legislation (Falkner et al. 2007). This partly reflects technical problems in transposition, and partly struggles by and within the French legal establishment (Mangenot 2005), but the existence of technical problems of transposition reflects a traditional French scepticism about implementing EU law. It appears that the SGAE's increased role in following transposition and changes in the balance of power within the French legal profession has improved the situation with regard to legislative compliance, but that does not mean that France does well or has lost its tendency, relative to the other states in this study or the EU as a whole, to forget transposition and implementation.

Departmental

As with all countries, the departmental level increases the difficulty of co-ordinating because the informational advantage enjoyed by each ministry justifies a relatively high degree of ministerial autonomy. Without the discipline of the Council vote and other formal institutions of the diplomatic level, the role of the central coordinators at the SGAE is much smaller.

When health policy is at the departmental level, the ministry is in the lead. It is the home of the technical civil servants who can assess the impact of EU policy ideas and who will often have ideas for their improvement, and it is the source of many of the experts and officials who represent France in all the various health policy forums, such as the High Level Group, Open Method of Co-ordination proceedings and the Platform on Diet, Nutrition and Physical Activity. French theory as well as practice emphasizes the formal distinction between departmental and diplomatic activity. In a given meeting of the High Level Group or the OMC, it is ministries speaking, not the French state. As with other states, the demands on central co-ordinators would be overwhelming if the SGAE and Permanent Representation had to be interested in every meeting across the EU. Further, the value they would add would be very low because, as generalists, they would be incompetent in specialized meetings of experts in agriculture, telecommunications or health.

The ministry seeks internal co-ordination in departmental affairs as well, which above all means more effort than other member states put into trying to keep officials from 'going native' in Brussels networks. The same ladder of people responsible for EU affairs, who are found quite far down in the bureaucratic hierarchy, leads to the ministry's co-ordinating unit. That unit nurtures the EU experts and tries to interest the rest of the ministry in its work, facilitates experts' trips to Brussels for EU committees and meetings, and identifies the French representatives and experts to attend meetings of groups such as the OMC or Platform on Diet, Nutrition and Physical Activity.

The co-ordination process means that the ministry officials and associated experts all know the French 'line' and might have clear guidance, both as an overspill from the high-level co-ordination and also because the presence of a European adviser in each ministerial

cabinet, and a ministry of health official in the Permanent Representation connect the ministries and the general French approach. The
problem of the French ministry is that like every other health ministry, it has a relatively parochial culture shot through with the techno-
cratic internationalism of scientists or other professionals. This
means that the international specialists can be an irritation to others,
one more group asking for time for issues whose importance might
not be clear. It also means that there is a permanent tendency for
there to be a gulf between international and line officials. There is
ultimately no way to get rid of the tension between EU knowledge
and health knowledge, or between time spent on the EU and time
spent on the health system itself (which might be easier to justify to
politicians). The French model invests relatively heavily in EU specialists within the health ministry and thereby tries to snuff out the
problem of officials who focus on substantive policy and undercut
diplomatic aims when they are in Brussels. In other words, it tries to
resist the centrifugal tendencies states experience at the departmental
and deliberative levels.

Deliberative

At the deliberative level, the lack of a European culture in the ministry dovetails with the relative weakness of non-state French lobbying, and, one interviewee said, a general lack of a 'European culture'
in France or at least French health policy. Compared to some countries (Germany, the Netherlands, the UK) or compared to the
French presence in other policy areas, the French are not very visible
or present at informal or semi-formal EU health policy events. This
is especially the case with events conducted in English. The effect of
common French non-participation in the broader Brussels health
policy debate is to heighten the centralization of French representation; the state is what speaks for France.

The traditional response is to rely on networks of French citizens
in the EU institutions. This is a well-developed system for placing
French citizens in important positions and keeping in touch with
them and is run out of the Permanent Representation and the
SGAE. In health, it has had some important members including a
long-lived Director of DG EMPL and the head of the Cabinet of the
Health Commissioner in 2008 (as other member state representatives
noted when I asked about French influence on health legislation).

But this kind of individual lobbying, however effective at steering
the Commission, has its limits in influencing broader debates. This

means that the lack of a general European culture in France creates problems at this level. No health ministry sends officials to every seminar and debate in Brussels; no health ministry would write the kinds of papers or lobby Commission officials in the way that works so well for lobbyists and experts at the deliberative level. French officials attend high-level conferences and participate in Brussels debates, but their ability to participate in the clash of ideas is limited by the special treatment that a representative of a member state will always receive (it is easy to watch: at public events, they are constantly approached by questioners trying to infer the state's thinking). The real problem is simply that French health organizations are, perhaps because of statism, and perhaps because of reluctance to lobby, not major actors in Brussels health lobbying. And statism at the deliberative level is always a problem.

Perhaps the issue that captures the strengths and weaknesses of the French approach to EU health policy is the issue of Services of General Interest. From the original Article 16 that underlies the concept to the continued prominence of the idea, France has been important in holding it up and promoting it as a general solution to a number of problems as diverse as utilities and health care regulation. An attractive idea, its political plausibility has often come from only two sources: DG Employment and Social Affairs (which otherwise cedes the internal market more completely) and France. Some interviewees from other countries laughed when I asked about the whole concept and made jokes about it being a French device to subsidize its giant utility companies. The idea lives on, largely thanks to France, but it is not winning the battle of ideas or setting the agenda. Again, that might be partly due to the weakness of the French outside of their state. Services of General Interest has a much harder time as a concept if it lives only at the diplomatic and occasionally departmental levels, simply because that is not where the clash of ideas happens in the EU. The clash of ideas is in the fluid and often time-wasting deliberative level, and that is where France is not very visible.

CONCLUSION: INFORMED, CO-ORDINATED, NIMBLE?

France demonstrates something simple but important: it is possible to develop a unified system that will have a worked-out position on almost everything and allow a high level of tactical action and strategic calculation, though it takes a great deal of management and work. The Ministry of Health has a chain of people working on EU issues that reaches further down its internal hierarchy than in any other state we studied, because that is required to gather information necessary to formulate a good dossier on any issue. The result is that French officials are less likely to 'go native' in Brussels, the French state has more knowledge of what the French are doing in Brussels, and the French develop a characteristic hard-bargaining style that some of their own EU specialists called 'arrogant' or even 'autistic' (Costa and Daloz 2005). Among other benefits, it means that France is unlikely to accidentally move favoured Commission agendas: the scarcity of significant initiatives during the French 2008 presidency was a sign not only of French scepticism about EU health policy, but also of French effectiveness at making sure it, rather than the Commission, controlled the agenda (as shown by the general agreement in the Council on its end of presidency statement on the Patient Mobility Directive).

The French weakness is, rather, in its reliance on formal, diplomatic and departmental methods on one hand and French networks on the other. This translates to a lack of influence on agenda-setting and the framing of debates, and reliance on high-level diplomatic interventions transparent (in Council) and opaque (lobbying the French head of the Health Commissioner's *cabinet* or important French officials in DG EMPL). This is something common to many member states, and a problem that, of the countries in this study, affects Spain badly. The difference is that a lack of French presence at deliberative levels is largely balanced out by its effectiveness at the diplomatic level. Interviewees from the EU institutions, the UK and Germany ranked it as tied with or close to the UK as the most effective member state. There might be questions about whether the broadly intergovernmentalist French approach is the best long-term approach or suited to shaping the basic parameters of EU health policy, but in the short term it unquestionably has an impact.

NOTES

1 The dilution of responsibilities and mandates entailed by such vague ministerial frontiers plays a role in explaining the occurrence of major public health scandals in France, such as blood contamination (Chevallier 2005; Morelle 1996; Steffen 2000).

2 'Le SGCI est donc un de ces lieux aux où se bricolent dans les routines du quotidien ces objects sacralisés ont pour nom "intérêt général", "volonté de l'État", "politique de France".' The appeal should be obvious (Eymeri 2002: 150).

8

GERMANY

If France is a famously hierarchical country, Germany is its political opposite. The German constitution was designed to make Germany a nation governed by consensus. Consensus government meant fragmentation: distributing power and autonomy through many parts of the state and different governments, and requiring them to work together to achieve anything. This meant federalism, with the federal states (Länder) autonomous but tightly integrated with the federation (Bund). It also meant a high degree of ministerial autonomy. This constitutional structure reinforces longstanding German traits of ministerial autonomy and territorial fragmentation. It produces a German paradox: intergovernmental co-ordination between federation and Länder in health can be better than intragovernmental co-ordination between health and other ministries.

It means, in EU health policy terms, that the German state does a good job of representing its federal nature, and that a ministry can sometimes be more active than a properly co-ordinated system would let it be. But that hardly seems like the recipe for the German 'success' in influencing European policy that many scholars see. In so far as that exists, it is because of German influence at the deliberative level of policy. That might be because Germany's health policy-making, which can look wasteful of human resources with its funds that cannot really compete or its Länder representatives doubling up with member states, but which is also an investment in EU-relevant skills and engagement.

SYSTEM AND STAKES

If France's signature style is intense internal politics and a glittering facade of unity, the German style is a combination of fragmentation, interconnection and consensus politics. German EU health policy engagement is profoundly shaped by that fragmentation and need for consensus, as is its exposure to EU policies.[1]

System

Like France, Germany has a social insurance system in which the system is funded mostly from payroll taxes. Unlike France, the German system has many different social insurance funds, each with an entrenched right to 'self-administration' (*selbstverwaltung*) (Klenk 2008: 145–190; Oberender et al. 2002). They have (very) slightly different menus of benefits: any competition is in the mere 2 per cent that are not mandatory. Their contribution rates are different, but after 2009 all funds will charge the same contribution measured as a percentage of income and will only be able to charge extra if the contributions are not enough to cover the benefits. Their ability to compete or diverge is further limited by risk-pooling that means funds cannot be punished for having poorer or more expensive members. While it is hard to identify the contribution of self-administration to any particular outcome in Germany politics, or much difference between funds, the existence of the distinctive level of autonomous insurance funds both adds actors to any German health policy debate and changes representation in the health care sector. The organizations might not be very autonomous in health care delivery and finance, but they are autonomous enough to influence the conduct of politics in Germany and even the EU.

German doctors are organized into medical organizations (one per Land), which play an important role in determining fees and practice in negotiation with the associations of funds. The Ärztekammern are the primary medical associations and all German physicians have to be a member of their respective Landesärztekammer. The medical associations that negotiate with the public sickness funds are called the Kassenärztliche Vereinigungen and represent only those physicians who participate in the public health care system. Both kinds of medical associations are organized at the level of the Länder and have head organizations at the federal level in Berlin. Hospitals are a mixture of municipal, charitable (often religious orders), university affiliated and private, the last category generally being former municipal hospitals that were sold by the local governments to a number of private chains. The Länder are involved in determining the number of hospital beds required for each specialty (hospital planning) and provide funds for hospital construction and equipment. The Länder are also responsible for public health, but public health in Germany is weak as a result of its misuses and the behaviour of many of its practitioners during the Nazi regime.

Stakes

The German health care system, like every European health care system, had to adapt to European Union patient mobility. But, because of the social insurance system, the initial adaptation was a mostly administrative challenge – developing procedures in case patients sought reimbursement for procedures for which they had not sought pre-authorization (Obermaier 2008a). Providers and regional authorities in areas near borders have a relatively long and pragmatic tradition of signing agreements on cross-border treatment, and interviewees in Germany (as in France) did not find the agreements very interesting or difficult. Furthermore, the diversity of funds means that they can often diffuse patient demands for services abroad by, for example, signing agreements with particular providers in other countries (Greer and Rauscher 2008).[2]

The first key vulnerability comes from the same purchaser–provider split that makes patient mobility less of a challenge. The problem is basically the same as that faced by France. As in other countries, the average length of stay and the number of hospital days have declined. As a result, fewer beds are needed. However, no politician is inclined to close down a popular municipal hospital providing health care close to people's homes and jobs. The result is policies of cross-subsidy or subsidy in the name of solidarity that interfere with competitive markets as EU law understands them. The second key vulnerability comes from the fact that Germany, uniquely in the EU, runs a fully substitutive private health insurance system that encourages high-status groups to opt out of the social insurance system and into the private system (the difference from other systems that permit private health insurance is that the privately insured do not have access to services via the social insurance system). This system was inegalitarian, and subsequent policies have threatened the privately insured with inclusion in, or risk-pooling with, the social system. Efforts to force risk-pooling are vulnerable to EU legal challenges because they roll back the role of the private sector (Thomson and Mossialos 2009).

For the German constitution, meanwhile, the stakes are back-door constitutional change. In Germany, the Länder are highly autonomous, important, powerful in their own right, and 'built into' the broader structure of German federalism through their participation in the Bundestag. They have an effective veto over most major German domestic policy. European integration initially disrupted this balance between federal and Land because EU affairs were a competency of the federation but increasingly affected Land competencies, such as hospitals and public health. Partly as a result, the Länder have been 'on the defensive' since the early 1990s (Sturm 2006: 47). Their strategy has been to use their considerable domestic political power in order to push the German federal government to take their interests into account. This basic effort to preserve the federal balance shapes German EU policy. Länder are, by the standards of European regional governments, large and sophisticated organizations. Even the smallest and least capable are able to assign a capable civil servant to each significant task, and basic prescriptions in the German constitution make it clear that the Länder must have influence over EU health policy.

EXPLAINING GERMANY'S EU HEALTH POLICY

'Consensus' is a simple word, but it can be difficult to grasp just how meaningful it is to describe a system as a 'consensus democracy'. Germany is such a consensus democracy, and it means that in even the smallest matters policymaking depends on bringing a large number of actors together, often at the earliest stages of agenda-setting. That wide distribution of power and vetoes led Peter Katzenstein (1987) to call Germany a 'semi-sovereign state', one in which political power is internally and externally constrained, and policymakers are bound together such that none can move until many move (Katzenstein 1987). It means that German EU policy is the accumulation of ministerial, unit and politicians' goals rather than the all-integrated strategic action that the French often try to create, and it means that German EU specialists are specialists in creating consensus in both the European and the German arenas.

Constitution

Federalism means that power is dispersed across multiple levels of government. In Germany, it also means that the different governments are highly interpenetrated. In Germany, unlike the other three countries in this study, the regional governments are 'built into' the central government, with a formal say in its decisions (Watts 1999, 2006). Only in rare cases does a single government make the decisions and implement the policies; it is much more common to find, for example, that the federal government passes legislation that the Länder must both approve in the Bundesrat and implement themselves. Without Länder agreement, the federal legislation might not pass, and without Länder effort it will not be implemented. As a result, German policy changes tend to be highly negotiated and slow, and German politics in practice is often the formation of consensus among a large number of groups and actors who could, if they so chose, block change.

In EU health policymaking, as in many other areas, federalism complicates issues. This comes through a simple and powerful injunction in the German constitution. While the federal government has an exclusive foreign affairs competency, Länder have a right to be consulted on any issue that touches their competencies. In health, this means all areas of public health. While the social funds are constitutionally classified as social security and are therefore an exclusive Bund competency, hospitals are under Länder control. As a result, most areas of health policy involve the Länder: EU reference networks, for example, or the Health Services Directive involve the Länder because they involve hospitals. This means that the Bundesrat, the German federal upper house in which the Länder sit, must agree to policies that affect Länder. The federal government, elected out of the lower house (Bundestag), must live with this.

Public administration

German fragmentation comes in two kinds: intergovernmental and interdepartmental. Intergovernmental fragmentation is part of the constitution. Interdepartmental fragmentation, within a given government, is also derived from a principle in the constitution. It is *Ressortprinzip*, which not only means ministerial responsibility – the activities of a ministry are the responsibility of the minister – but also means ministerial autonomy. Subject to the *Kanzlerprinzip* and *Rechtlinienprinzip* of the constitution, which empower the Chancellor to steer overall policy, ministers are legally free to do what they want (Rudzio 2006: 261–269). Naturally, party loyalty, party connections and party leaders limit divergence, but on the lower level it means that everyday, active co-ordination is rare. The result, unsurprisingly, is that ministries often diverge.

Intragovernmental fragmentation comes with and is underpinned by the relatively small number of generalists in the German civil services; most people in a health or economics ministry have been in that ministry for most of their careers. German civil servants are mostly educated in law, and are accustomed to a high degree of autonomy. There is a small top set of advisers surrounding a minister; some civil service interviewees in different ministries recommended that I speak with a ministerial adviser, and joked that if I learned what he or she was thinking, I should let the officials know.

Traditionally, this meant a country often led by its officials (in the homeland of Max Weber). With a high degree of departmental autonomy and weak central co-ordination, bureaucratic dominance of information, a civil service seen as elite and only intermittent political control, German bureaucrats and departmental units often had great autonomy. German politicians have slowly fought back, diversifying their sources of expertise and building central co-ordinating units that are more politically responsive (Goetz 2007). These are trends seen in many countries with traditional strong bureaucracy, but the extent of German fragmentation was greater than most of them.

This shift is slow in EU policymaking. In dealing with the EU, writes Klaus Goetz (2007):

> the executive dominates vis-à-vis other participants in the policy process; the attention of the political executive is highly selective, thereby creating both considerable space for bureaucratic agenda-setting and conditions for weak political controls; policy processes are strongly sectorised; and EU policy coordination is weakly developed . . . as EU integration still largely advances on the basis of 'integration through law', legal expertise, as the traditional key skill of the Federal bureaucracy, remains highly valued.
>
> (Goetz 2007: 166)

Goetz doubts that it will last, but it is a fair description of German EU health policymaking nowadays (see also Dyson 2003).

Health ministry

German health ministries and their ministers are traditionally weak, especially compared to the might of ministries such as economics. This is partly because health care has not been traditionally seen as much of a problem in Germany. But it is mostly because they do not directly run much. Unlike the UK's Department of Health and devolved ministries, or the Spanish regional health ministries, the federal ministry has few responsibilities for actual service delivery. The low profile of the ministry also allowed Social Democrat Ulla Schmidt, who was appointed in January 2001, to become (as of late 2008) the longest serving health minister in the EU. This allowed her to develop greater personal networks and mastery of EU health policy debates than most other ministers could hope to enjoy.

Ministries everywhere become more important when they control major laws, staff resources or money. There are not many major health laws (and major health reforms are so high profile as to be directed by the Chancellor) and a ministry without a health service naturally lacks resources or money. Those are in the hands of the various social insurance funds, professional organizations and agencies. As a result, the health ministry is competent (in both senses of the word) in fairly high-level supervision of the system, and can take a strategic view of the German health care system, but it has relatively limited power either over health system actors such as funds or over other ministries. Key relationships in German health care are outside its purview.

GERMANY'S EU MODEL IN HEALTH

Germany's ability to be an active and engaged EU member state is reduced by its complexity and need for internal consensus that slows it at the diplomatic level. Simply put, the kind of strategic action that France can indulge is hard because Germany invests a great deal of time in developing its own internal consensus, and because the consensus is necessarily relatively rigid.

That does not help explain relative German success in influencing EU policy, a success other observers have noted (Anderson 1997; Bulmer 1997; Dyson and Goetz 2003). There are two reasons for this success. One is that intragovernmental co-ordination is not such a problem at the important departmental level. While Germany might never appear as the kind of strategic actor that the French, British or even Spanish routinely try to be, it can be perfectly effective at the departmental level where most EU politics are just as sectoral as German public administrations, if not more. The other is the strength of Germans, and perhaps Germany, at the deliberative level. The sheer number of Germans engaged in Brussels increase the likelihood that somebody with knowledge of German conditions is at the table.

Diplomatic

The formal organization of German EU policymaking is more complex than its day-to-day operations. As with most member states, the international unit of the federal health ministry is the nexus between the line ministry and EU issues. Mostly based in Berlin, it communicates directly with the Permanent Representation, where the ministry has some staff posted. It has to work closely with the Länder, each of which has a person (or at least a fraction of a person) working on health in Brussels and in its own capital. The Länder assign a civil servant to follow each federal official to EU events. They also have committees on each EU subject area, with standing chairs as well as rapporteurs who are designated when there is an EU legislative proposal. In German consensus-oriented fashion, they check and balance: if the chair of the Bundestag committee is from one of the major parties, the civil servant accompanying the federal official and the rapporteurs on major reports will generally come from another major party (above all, this balances Social Democrats and Christian Democrats and reflects the fact that parties are the most important Bundesrat division). In a grand coalition (Christian Democrats and Social Democrats) such as currently governs Germany, this balancing continues but the two big parties, which between them dominate the Länder, are less likely to veto each other's ideas. The Bundesrat agrees the eventual position; after the subject committee reports, the European Affairs committee decides the position that is put to the whole Bundesrat. Once it is decided, it is rigid; while the German government can still override or interpret the Bundesrat decision, it is far too time-consuming to go back and start over.

On paper this is a two-stage process in which the Länder, who thanks to documents and their civil servant know as much as the Bund, agree a position and then negotiate a shared position with the Bund. In reality it tends to be much less formal. This allows the art of consensus politics to work; for example, the federal officials involved in formulating a position on the Patient Mobility Directive, already known and trusted as individuals, reached out very early to the Länder and were invited to address a Länder conference on the subject.[3] That naturally influences Länder positions.

Intergovernmental fragmentation appeared to be much less of a problem than interdepartmental fragmentation. In intergovernmental co-ordination, all sorts of hierarchies and formal relationships dissolve in the reality of emails, meetings and a relatively egalitarian culture. It appears that this success comes from four sources. First, the law and power relationships underpinning the relationship are egalitarian. The Länder have to be involved. It is illegal for the Bund to forget the Länder. Second, the people constantly interact; their ministries are usually not very interested in EU affairs, and their governments are not always very interested in their health ministries, and so they can work on developing their relationships and joint working in the absence of major political tensions (unlike their Spanish counterparts). It is also easier because there are few engaged in Länder–Bund co-ordination in health in Germany, and some have had extremely longstanding relationships. So trust and informality can ease co-ordination. Third, this co-ordination takes place against a backdrop of a consensus-oriented German political culture. We could attribute this to any kind of cultural trait, but it is simpler to point out that in an institutional environment as complex and interpenetrated as Germany, nothing would get done without a high level of consensus. So if the Bund office is overstretched and willing to cede the first draft to a Land, there is usually a Land, usually a big Land with capacity, to write the first draft. Given the importance of the first draft, and explanatory memoranda, this is a sign of confidence and a high-trust environment. It also means, of course, that the bigger Länder that can afford to put more effort in (i.e. reduce other burdens on the responsible officials) have more influence. That means Bavaria, Baden-Württemberg and North Rhine-Westphalia. Fourth and finally, relative to other issues in Germany, EU affairs have to work reasonably well because the EU sets the agenda and the timetable. It is not a good idea to have longrunning squabbles because that would mean Germany would be unable to participate in EU decisions.

*Intra*governmental co-ordination is a different matter. British, French and Spanish interviewees, as well as Commission officials, commented on how the frustration of dealing with Germany usually comes from its inability to agree lines between ministries rather than between Bund and Länder in any given policy area. Ministerial autonomy means that, famously, Germany can have multiple contradictory positions and not even know it. At the end, when some co-ordination is required if a country is to vote in a Council and when disagreeing ministries learn what they are doing, Germany is famous for not voting ('abstention is the German vote', fumed one interviewee), although Council proceedings generally mask abstention along with opposition.

This ministerial autonomy comes with relatively weak central co-ordination (Jeffery and Paterson 2004: 70). The Chancellor can, of course, override ministers, as Art. 65 makes clear, and a call from the Chancellor's office can put an end to ministerial adventuring. But the routine co-ordination carried out by the French SGAE or British Cabinet Office European Secretariat is not present, and ministries do not turn out to voluntarily contact each other that much (whether for strategic reasons, or because of time pressures, or because they do not know who to contact, or because they do not see the point). The German Permanent Representation, which (like the French Permanent Representation) is staffed at the working level by officials posted from the ministries (in this case, health), is not set up to catch divergence systematically (and counsellors posted from different departments might not have reason to).

If ministries can 'hide', something that is much easier in Germany than in France, then sometimes they will. It can be rational for a weaker ministry (such as health) to let issues develop in Brussels until they have a momentum of their own and cannot be blocked by a stronger ministry. If participating in co-ordinating mechanisms means letting an opposed ministry decide policy, then a little less co-ordination might be entirely rational. This could not happen on any significant level in the UK or France because the SGAE and the Cabinet Office European Secretariat exist to pick up such divergence (backed up by those countries' foreign ministries) and because those countries' bureaucratic cultures punish such efforts to bypass co-ordination.

Departmental

At this level we again see the mechanisms that produce the German paradox of intergovernmental co-ordination and intragovernmental fragmentation. Germans in the OMC or High Level Group are not there *as* the German state (in the way that ministers are in Council meetings), but they still *represent* the German state, and are accordingly just as tightly integrated with the Länder. The basic pattern is the same: all the papers go to the Länder as well as the Bund. Länder (through their committees and delegated officials) and federation produce a joint statement, whether by reconciling different papers they originally wrote, or by amicably going through multiple drafts of the same paper. As usual, amity is more efficient because they eventually have to agree on something, and efficiency is improved by the officials' experience with each other and the system of nominating individual Länder to represent all the Länder.

This starts to explain the puzzle of how Germany can so routinely have difficulty with central co-ordination and yet be such an influential actor in EU politics. The German health ministry, in a fragmented system, need not be any less influential than the French. It can still draw on a considerable level of resources (somewhat multiplied by working with the Länder, somewhat divided by the need to co-ordinate with them) (Gunlicks 2003: 347). Intragovernmental fragmentation might occasionally help at this level, as it means that the German health ministry is more likely to represent interests of its sector rather than a compromise worked out elsewhere. Of course, the problem is that because so much EU health policy does not come from DG Sanco or EPSCO, the departmental level of the Ministry of the Economy or other similar ministries might be creating problems that will later rebound on health. But the health sector, in the mean time, might reflect a considerable amount of German influence.

It also points back to the question of what it means to do consensus politics well. If the Germany health ministry eventually comes to a clash with the finance ministry – let alone one noticed by ministers – it will probably lose. So good practice, explained one high-level federal official, is to take steps at the very start of any major issue to bring the other interested ministries on board. That eases tensions and, if possible, keeps real policy conflicts from becoming bad-humoured. If conflict is likely, a good German official will make sure to have the minister informed and in agreement before starting an interministerial consultation. That style of consensus politics works well in the EU, where soft skills and consensus-building are often required to take any action.

Deliberative

A second part of the reason for German influence is that Germans lobby more than most countries; as Chapter 5 noted, Germany and the UK are among the countries whose interest groups are particularly likely to join EU groups while France and Spain, along with the other Mediterranean countries and the 2004 accession states, are less likely to join groups that lobby the EU. If we are to count interest groups such as NGOs and professions, then Germany is very active, even when the German state is not. That is partly a function of the design of the German health care system. Many of the associations and insurance funds have the extra resources to lobby on their own, and some do. One interviewee, from a German sickness fund, pointed to precisely this wider distribution of politically useful resources as an advantage of the German system (October 2008).

German federalism adds to the numbers. Every Land office in Brussels has a representative from its ministry responsible for health (or ministries, since some divide between public health, part of the environment ministry, and health services, which are associated with social services). That is a workforce of perhaps two dozen Land representatives in Brussels who follow at least the most prominent health policies. EU expertise most often comes from previous experience with the EU, and the German system diffuses that widely.

CONCLUSION: INFORMED, CO-ORDINATED, NIMBLE?

It might be telling that, in response to detailed questions about process, the German interviewees, unlike the others, constantly discussed influence in terms of drafting reports and writing the initial statements of opinion. This probably flows naturally from a consensus-oriented system; the first draft sets the agenda.

Writing and agreeing those drafts takes time because consensus politics takes time and because respect between governments takes time. Germany, as many interviewees said, expends much of its effort on building its own internal consensus instead of being able to 'sell a line' six months before the legislation, as the UK official recommended. That is time not spent lobbying and shaping debates in Brussels. Individual Germans do a great deal of influencing, and many policy areas of the EU show marked German influence, but Germany as a member state is often invisible at even the diplomatic, Council level. Co-ordination – even the largely amicable and productive relationship between the Bund and Länder in health – takes up time and resources that could do something else. Several German interviewees spoke rather wistfully of the quality of briefing they see on the side of France or the UK: no matter the issue, they said, the British and the French had briefings, prepared positions, arguments and facts at their fingertips. They, at least, blamed the German need to devote resources to internal co-ordination.

Germany also shares the common problem of a low level of engagement with the EU in health departments. Explaining EU policy issues to other health ministry officials is hard; forwarding dozens of boring emails about EU issues can annoy other officials (and Germany was one of the countries for which interviewees spoke about the challenge of informing line officials without irritating them). The international unit of the federal health ministry must work to induce colleagues to help them with impact assessment, policy formulation or even wish lists. This problem is worse at the Land level. Land departments' strength and weakness is their local focus; the EU can seem very distant, and even for things that unquestionably matter (such as state aids to hospitals or the Working Time Directive) the complexity of EU engagement and its low salience might make it more rational to do something else. Officials engage as they gain EU experience (which the German system diffuses relatively broadly) or as they face shocks such as the Working Time Directive, Services Directive and currently patient mobility legislation. But of course influence works best before, rather than, after, a shock of that sort.

The Federal Republic of Germany has a long and articulate tradition of complaint about federalism, and a long and tortured history of trying to reform it (Scharpf 1988; Scharpf et al. 1976). EU health policymaking, at least, shows no signs of being one of the areas of greatest trouble, in large part because of large areas of substantive agreement and because of the good working relationships between the relatively stable cadre of people who work in the field. Germany shows how a small network of people can make the complicated relatively simple if they are bound by trust and mutual respect. But admiring that trust between regional and state government officials is not enough. They work together because they must. That is a key point about the structure of EU relations, and states more broadly. Germany has a system based on what is essentially legal equality between the Länder and the Bund, underpinned by veto power. From that basis, much co-operation is possible and takes place. So we have two poles, one of hierarchy and one of egalitarianism. France demonstrates the power and effectiveness of hierarchy as a tool to influence EU policy. Germany demonstrates the power of legal equality and consensus as tools to preserve an established constitutional balance under threat from the EU's growing competencies (and its unexpected deliberative benefits in distributing experience and knowledge of EU affairs widely). The next two countries, the UK and Spain, are both in motion between these two poles, and show different ways of working out the tensions between the EU, domestic policymaking and their constitutions.

NOTES

1   An extremely good work on German politics in the EU context is Sturm and Pehle (2006).
2   This takes advantage of the introduction of Article 140e into the Social Code Book V in 2004 as a response to ECJ rulings.
3   The same German official who was invited to work with the Länder on their report was rightly also proud of the fact that after only a few months on the job, his Finnish counterparts invited him to the sauna – a serious sign of respect and friendship for Finns. A better example of the usefulness and transferability of consensus-building and networking skills is hard to imagine.

9

THE UNITED KINGDOM

If France and Germany are political opposites, France and the UK are much closer to being twins than either might like to remark. Both have strongly unitary political cultures and political traditions suspicious of constraint on their sovereignty. They are the two member states that traditionally seek unified EU policies of all kinds. The difference is that the UK, on a day-to-day basis, is less internally hierarchical and fractious. The top British civil service is classically a network, or 'village' (Heclo and Wildavsky 1974). That is because Whitehall, as it is known, is still mostly a unified civil service body; despite the growth of special advisers attached to ministers, the top levels of British administration are still dominated by generalists from a single corps of officials with a strong culture of active information sharing. If anything, this should make British co-ordination smoother and friendlier, with the civil service smoothing out undesired policy contradictions (i.e. policy contradictions not worth fighting out) and political disagreements clearly set out for presentation to the right Cabinet committee. But Whitehall is changing, with less territorial unity since devolution and a slow but steady reduction in the role of classical Whitehall civil servants in health policy. The UK has done relatively well at using a network to attain the co-ordination and unity that the French do with hierarchy. The question is whether that network is changing and whether it is capable of dealing with the new pressures on it.

SYSTEM AND STAKES

The UK health systems are, like Spain, national health services in a decentralized country. National health systems create a tight relationship between the health sector and the state, because both finance health out of general taxation. Before 1998 the UK combined political unity under one government with 'administrative devolution' for Northern Ireland, Scotland and Wales. This meant that there were separate Northern Ireland, Scottish and Welsh health systems, with separate ministers, some scope for policy divergence and considerable scope for divergent implementation; 1999 saw political devolution, in which the departments responsible for health and other services in the three areas were matched by new legislatures. These legislatures have considerable ability to diverge, and their politics and policies do. This means that the differences between UK health systems can be large enough to matter in an EU context (Greer 2004, 2007a) and that its four elected governments might choose to disagree on issues including EU policy stances.

System

Just as Germany is usually treated as the ideal type of a social insurance system, the UK is usually taken as the ideal type of a national health insurance system (it is telling that the two kinds of systems are named after statesmen of the two countries: Bismarck and Beveridge).[1] In the UK's National Health Service systems, the government directly owns hospitals and employs specialist doctors and many others; it contracts with independent practitioners for primary care; and it finances the whole health care system out of general taxation. Care is, as a much repeated motto goes, 'free and universal at the point of service', which means that there is only one effective tool to ration resources: the UK's infamous elective surgery waiting lists. The result is highly redistributive and popular, and yet a subject of much grumbling by people who are left waiting for treatment by the cost containment and clinical priorities.

That identifies the first vulnerability of the UK systems, one that applies to any national health system that provides care for free out of general taxation (and to a lesser extent to any system that rations by waiting). Once the European Court of Justice made it clear in *Watts* that its patient mobility decisions extended to the UK and other national health systems without reimbursement mechanisms, it emerged that the specific problem for this kind of system would hinge on waiting. Specifically, how long should a patient have to wait before he or she could go to a different EU provider and seek reimbursement from the NHS? The Court, of course, phrased it in the reverse: what, other than protectionism, justifies long NHS waiting lists when providers from other EU states are eager to treat the patients? In *Watts*, the Court's answer was: nothing.

So while it shied away from specifying the concept of an unacceptable wait, it made it clear that the NHS could not use with impunity its traditional rationing mechanism of sending people to NHS facilities where they would have to wait. UK officials were not impressed with the case or the logic of the decisions:

> There are basically three ways to ration: by co-payments, by limited lists of service, and by waiting lists. The judges in Luxembourg understand the first two much better than the idea of waiting.
>
> (UK official, August 2005)

> The way the debate has developed is that it is easier for social insurance countries to accommodate ECJ – the cases came through that route – and, dare one say it, that's what the judges understand.
>
> (UK official, March 2006)

All four UK governments already have some form of 'patient choice' that allows patients to seek a different hospital, whether immediately (as in England) or after a wait (as in Wales) and patients seem to appreciate it, but rank it low as a priority. But there is a difference between a level of choice chosen by the systems and a level of choice chosen by the ECJ.

Stakes

For years the UK argued, reasonably, that it was exempt from the EU jurisprudence on patient mobility and much else because it was a national health system without payments by procedure. This was a reasonable interpretation of EU law but just as unacceptable to the Court as the German or French insistence that *Kohll* and *Decker* did not apply to them; all the member states had focused on the particular issue (reimbursement) instead of the Court's steady application of internal market law to health. In *Watts*, the Court replied that it had mechanisms for charging foreigners, so charging was possible (and anyway, the development of a system for payment by procedure, oddly called Payment by Results, was rapidly invalidating the argument). *Watts* made it clear that the NHS systems fell under patient mobility law, although the exact meaning of this depends on the meaning given to the Court's ruling that clinical needs, rather than finance, should dictate when a patient has waited unacceptably long and can or should go abroad.

Devolution means that the stakes of EU health policy are somewhat different from system to system (Greer 2004, 2009c). The standout is the English NHS, which is directly run by the UK government. Under Prime Minister Tony Blair, and subsequently Gordon Brown, the UK moved the English NHS explicitly toward a model in which the government funds the health care system but patient choice increasingly dictates resource flows and provision is competitive and open to private and non-profit firms as well as increasingly independent NHS providers. In this market model, there is a great deal of vulnerability to competition, state aids and public procurement law because all three are bases for legal challenge by disappointed bidders. In an effort to make their market more competitive, and to defend against the inevitable lawsuits, English policymakers have erected defences against challenge by forcing the English NHS to comply with EU public procurement law (interviews, DH and former minister, July 2008). The market might or might not be implemented (and it seems that we have already passed the high water mark of the reforming spirit) but its legal consequences and effects on EU exposure are separate from whether it changes patients' experiences. If nothing else, there is no legal or practical effort to take the tack that the French and the Germans have taken, which is to argue that their health sectors are not full-scale markets. The English have taken the challenge: to make their country compatible with a large part of internal market law (Greer and Rauscher 2008).

Paradoxically, this might put the three devolved systems in some danger. All three use the private sector to various degrees (although none of them has forged ahead in the English manner, and each of the three has somewhere rolled back private involvement in provision). But once the UK's litigants, non-public providers, courts and competition authorities are sensitized to the variety of EU rules that can be used to argue with health ministries, it is highly likely that they will start to demand that the devolved health care systems conform. We cannot predict their success, but it means that the three devolved systems must do as much 'Europe-proofing' as the more adventurous English NHS policymakers. It also means that the UK does not provide a united front; it remains to be seen what happens if somebody challenges a Scottish private contracting decision (of which there are still many) in the UK competition tribunal on the grounds that Scotland is ignoring the UK's interpretation of EU law.[2]

Constitutionally, the stakes are the same as the Germans and Spanish face. As a decentralized state, the UK also faces the risk of constitutional change through the back door. The UK government, in its policies for the English NHS, has pulled the rug out from under Scotland if Scotland's government wants to argue that a national health system such as it operates is exempt from parts of EU law. Unlike Germany, the UK's regional participation in EU policy depends on goodwill and does not include formal equality or inter-governmental vetoes.

EXPLAINING THE UK'S EU HEALTH POLICY

The UK is, again, like France in its strongly unitary political culture. The doctrine was called 'parliamentary supremacy' and meant that the UK Parliament in Westminster was supreme and sovereign. EU membership obviously vitiates much of that, but unity and autonomy for the government live on in London and the UK state.

The UK's unitary culture therefore shares France's problems of relating general rules to specific circumstances, for example, coping with EU legislation. France historically created legal exceptions for various groups or opportunistically failed to implement some rules. The UK simply ignored a wide variety of local differentiation amidst a general management culture that gave tremendous autonomy to professions, corporate groups such as universities, and local units of all sorts (Bulpitt 1983; Greer 2006c; Moran 2003). Over time, the UK has become more centralized, with more efforts (especially in England) to make local actors accountable to the centre with reporting, reduction in local autonomy and the role of local government, and a variety of new public management techniques. At least in principle, this transmits EU law quickly and effectively through, without shock absorbers.

Of course, the UK is also distinctive among EU states (and our four states) in its historic and present level of anti-EU public opinion. The presentation of the EU in British politics is often very negative, and public opinion is markedly, and consistently, anti-EU (Baisnée 2005; Díez Medrano 2000). This is why it was a relief for the UK government to have the French, Dutch and then Irish torpedo the constitution and its Lisbon descendant; it spared them a potential lost referendum. But it produces the UK's paradox: one of the EU's most effective member states is the one with the most hostile public opinion.

Constitution

France, Germany and Spain, like most countries, have written constitutions that collect their fundamental constitutional rules, and the rules for changing them, into one document. The UK, along with Israel and New Zealand, does not have a written constitution; it has a combination of laws and precedents agreed to be 'constitutional'. This permits small changes and adaptation over time; in the favourite phrase, it allows the British political system to muddle through. Devolution is a classic case of such muddling, because today's devolution legislation is a solution to the specific territorial political problems of the 1990s rather than an overarching design for stability. Those problems were mostly to do with the application of Conservative policy in Scotland and Wales, where the Conservatives did not have a majority. As a civil servant joked to me, 'Thatcher put the "Great" back in Britain but took the "United" out of Kingdom'.

Devolution therefore shielded Northern Ireland, Scotland and Wales from English policy by creating their own governments. It also created a complicated set of asymmetries (Hazell and Rawlings 2005; Trench 2005, 2007, 2008):

- The UK government, elected in UK general elections, is the 'federal' government for foreign affairs, defence, EU policy and similar state responsibilities.
- The UK government also directly governs England, so its health department is both the 'federal' department for issues such as dealing with the WHO and the department responsible for politics and policy for the English NHS.
- The UK government does *not* have the authority to pass laws that bind the four UK systems to similar standards or procedures.
- The UK government is also responsible for most tax bases and for the budgets that fund the devolved governments. While there are extensive statements of funding policy, they are not laws and are within the power of the UK government.
- On the other hand, the standard formula it has used to fund the devolved governments has been a block formula that permits them

to spend their budgets on what they like, so the financial spending power has not meant interference.

- Scotland has 'primary legislative competency', which means that it can pass laws in any area not explicitly reserved to the UK government. This includes almost all legislation for health policy.
- Wales has 'secondary' legislative competency, which means that it can implement and innovate within primary legislation passed at Westminster. Wales is also in the midst of a very complicated transition to a more autonomous position, a transition that might not go as expected.
- Northern Ireland is bound into a complicated set of 'East–West' (UK) and 'North–South' (Northern Ireland and Republic of Ireland) obligations and constraints, and has fewer powers because of its peculiar politics, but has a great deal of legal autonomy in health.
- Finally, in principle devolution does not constrain the powers of Westminster, so in theory the Westminster Parliament (read: UK government) could amend any part of the law of devolution. Doing so would be a constitutional change, but the real costs that might deter governments would be political ones.

One of the problems with muddling through is that it is hard to tell when you can stop muddling. The very flexibility of the UK means that almost anything can be a pretext for proposals for constitutional change. The costs of changing the Spanish or German, or even the much amended French, constitutions are very high, and it is clear when change is happening. The UK is less able to resist the various cross-cutting pressures for constitutional change that come from the various contradictions (for example, Scotland can define any level of social citizenship that it likes, but the Treasury in London determines whether it can pay for it). The effect is that it is always hard to gauge the effects of intergovernmental tensions; potentially anything, including small spats about EU policy, can become fuel for an intergovernmental conflagration (Greer and Trench 2008). All it takes is for one government or the other to be careless or incendiary.

Since 2007, when Labour lost control of Scotland and was forced into coalition in Wales, the devolved governments have defied the most dramatic expectations of conflict. The Scottish National Party (SNP) has sought to maintain calm intergovernmental relations overall while selectively picking fights, and in Wales the nationalists of Plaid Cymru are in coalition with Labour and therefore unlikely to attack it. London has been less astute, but that primarily means it ceded the agenda to the devolved governments. That situation is a creature of current political strategies; any election in the UK could change the willingness of the various parties to maintain their relatively unified and technical, if low-capacity, EU health networks.

Public administration

Whitehall, the UK's civil service, is just as much an ideal type of public administration as the French or German. It is so studied, copied and admired (not least by interviewees in this project) for its attractive combination of attributes: a non-partisan civil service at the very top as well as the bottom, with the department leadership and ministerial office in the hands of civil servants; careers in the civil service that allow it to recruit and retain top-quality candidates; internal promotion that maintains its autonomy; generalism that prevents German-style fragmentation; and a strong esprit de corps.[3]

At least on paper, an organization with these attributes would do a superb job of co-ordinating EU policy. It would have good-quality people with a shared, general, approach that diminished fragmentation and enhanced communication within what some observers called the 'Whitehall village' (Heclo and Wildavsky 1974). It would muster bonds of trust and communication networks within the civil service in order to produce this co-ordination without hierarchy or the explicit level of political involvement found in France. The independent Northern Irish Civil Service (Carmichael 2002) and the separate foreign service fit with the dominant culture. Indeed, the UK is known in academic literature (Page 2005) and my interviews for its relatively good level of co-ordination (interviewees from the three other countries and the EU institutions spontaneously offered up that they had great respect for the UK civil service).

Being more co-ordinated than Spain is not enough for Whitehall's many critics. When not pointing out its failings in delivery and confused political accountability (Lodge and Rogers 2006), they often task it with precisely the failure to 'join up' government. Most countries have seen the 'demystification of high bureaucratic office', with top officials getting less respect and deference from politicians and citizens (Page and Wright 2007). In the UK, it has led to officials agreeing with their political superiors that the proper role of Whitehall departments is 'delivery', i.e. the effective design and execution of policies determined by the politicians. This is strange, historically; it gives responsibility for delivery to officials in departments that have historically always relied on delegation to units such as local government or NHS boards, while it gives responsibility for policy-making to the most under-resourced political elites of our four countries (Page 2007). But it seems to be the direction of travel, for now and for the foreseeable future (Greer 2008b).

This public administration, however strong the tendencies to fragmentation might be, comes with a strongly unitary political culture. It is simply not in Whitehall's culture to condone the kind of ministerial hide-and-seek that Germany sometimes sees. Endless interdepartmental meetings might annoy politicians, but they reflect the comparatively strong ability of the British civil servants to find, if not always resolve, intragovernmental conflict. Nor is disunity in Westminster's culture or the devolved governments; divergence from the government line is cause for dismissal in British politics, and politicians generally do agree on salient issues as a question of self-preservation as well as ideological selection. That might be an attractive level of unity at an attractive cost, but there are many who point out that the UK could do better: 'Joined-up government', as a goal, had its day early in the twenty-first century, but the objective of total co-ordination still lives on and seems achievable in the UK in a way that other countries might consider utopian (Bogdanor 2005). Whitehall's unitary culture is probably why.

Health ministry

The Department of Health is the line ministry with two sets of responsibilities. One is for the management and policy of the National Health Service in England. This job overwhelmingly dominates the department; no other ministry in Europe has a problem as immense as directly running a health service for 55 million people. So the DH might better be called DENHS: Department of the English NHS. The other job is as a UK department, responsible for the work of the UK government in health. Given that public health and health services are overwhelmingly devolved to Northern Ireland, Scotland and Wales, that means little more than EU and international relations (Lodge and Mitchell 2006) though the devolved governments will often buy into DH programmes. The departments responsible for health in Northern Ireland, Scotland and Wales share the preoccupation with running health services and have even fewer resources dedicated to international work (none of them have full-time health department officials dedicated to EU issues).

Of the four member states, the UK has the most powerful health department. Remembering that political power usually means laws, resources and money, the fact that the Secretary of State for Health, the top health minister, runs an organization with over 1 million contracted or employed staff and a large part of discretionary spending makes it an important job. It is also politically salient; the political pressure around health in the UK is enormous and was particularly impressive under Tony Blair. While there are still more influential ministerial positions, health ranks high and can make a strong case for itself in intragovernmental spats. In Scotland and Wales, health is important for the same reasons; more important, in fact, because there is no taxation, war or benefits, and not much economic management, to compete with it. Northern Ireland is a different case, with its politicians traditionally avoiding the health portfolio. Northern Ireland voters might care about health but vote on other issues, and so a health portfolio can mean quite a lot of grief without an opportunity to win votes. The difference is that the devolved departments are much smaller and spread work out very thinly: one Scottish health department official I interviewed in 2005 had 14 work streams, only one of them EU related (and he had been suggested to me as a particularly EU-engaged official by one of his superiors!).

Reflecting the total imbalance between its roles as a UK department and an English health department, the DH is organized and staffed itself to run English health services rather than make the UK's EU policy. Few of the top officials of the DH are the traditional Whitehall officials of UK politics textbooks. Instead, they are NHS managers, health professionals and outside hires (Greer and Jarman 2007a, 2007b). This changing in staffing, and the priorities it bespeaks, have two effects for EU policy. One is that they lack the networks and (often poorly defined) skills of traditional civil servants, much of which are to do with sharing information and handling interdepartmental relations. The other, as a devolution official from the Ministry of Justice noted about the DH in an October 2006 conversation about devolution and health policy, is that 'managers don't mind inefficiency so long as it's on somebody else's budget'. This might be a good orientation for a task-oriented manager, but it does not suggest that the very top level and the management tiers, as against the expert International Division, will be good long-term EU chess players.

THE UK'S EU MODEL IN HEALTH

The UK's model of European Union affairs, which like every state it is simply generalizing to health policy, puts an emphasis on co-ordination but does not use as much hierarchy (Bulmer and Burch 1998). Whitehall is hierarchical – it is a government bureaucracy, after all – but its structure reflects its older make-up as a unified, career, generalist, socially homogeneous organization. In other words, it presumes a high level of trust and puts less emphasis on subject expertise than on good procedure. It remains to be seen whether the changes in the civil service, especially the prominence of NHS managers in the top tiers of the DH, undermine this model. The International Division of the DH, UKREP and the Cabinet Office European Secretariat, at least, make up a good example of Whitehall working well. The result is that the UK can reduce the costs of co-ordination and information gathering by having a higher level of trust and less political engagement. The question is whether this can survive other reforms, such as devolution, and the turn to delivery in the senior civil service.

Diplomatic

One of the characteristics of the UK model of EU policy is that it tries particularly hard to 'mainstream' issues by making line officials responsible for the European Union aspects of their work. An official in Leeds (the administrative headquarters of the English NHS) or one of the DH offices spread across South London, runs the logic, is far better equipped to deal with his or her technical issues than a generalist in the International Division of the Department of Health. With some briefing and logistical support from the DH (and perhaps the Permanent Representation), that official is trusted to argue, or at least help formulate, the UK's position. The International Division of the DH has the diplomatic skills and leads the effort to 'mainstream' EU affairs in the DH by transferring responsibility to the knowledgeable line officials. The idea is that they should go to EU meetings and formulate UK positions as much as possible, with the International Division and the central co-ordinating bodies keeping an eye out only for complex problems or contradictions in the developing UK line. This level of trust and active information sharing is remarkable, and partly possible because of confidence in UK traditions of very active information sharing, copying everybody relevant into every communication.

The hub of the UK EU machine is the Cabinet Office European Secretariat. The Cabinet Office is the centre of government, and its co-ordinating roles mean that its officials get responses more quickly and fully than almost any others. The European Secretariat is one of the most important parts of the Cabinet Office, and carries out the traditional role of a Cabinet Office unit. Its role is to apply its traditional skills to the formulation of EU policy, namely to identify emerging issues and emerging departmental 'lines', identify contradictions and convene an escalating series of forums to resolve contradictions and prepare a UK line (starting with email or phone calls, running through official to ministerial committees, and on paper eventually ending in Cabinet, or at least a decision by the Prime Minister and inner circle). As they are copied into essentially every piece of paper or email of importance, their routine co-ordinating ability is impressive. Departmental divergences tend to be the product of unresolved political divergence, and in such situations the European Secretariat will use its series of meetings to force decisions.

Then, in Brussels, there is the UKREP – the Permanent Representation. The Permanent Representation takes its like from the Cabinet Office European Secretariat, from the Foreign and Commonwealth Office (which runs it), and very high levels of politics, but communicates directly with the DH and other line departments. In most routine cases, that means the European Secretariat is only generally aware of a line created in the DH and put forth by UKREP and visiting DH officials. In more political cases, there will be a decision orchestrated by the European Secretariat for UKREP to put forth. UKREP also puts a great deal of effort into lobbying, and is generally highly active. The UK is again like France: it is line ministry officials and the permanent representation that try to shape opinions in Brussels, while the co-ordinators in the capital mostly co-ordinate and develop strategies.

This is an impressive machine, one admired by most countries that deal with the UK. The problem is that the Whitehall machine has not adapted to devolution, and it has not adapted to devolution because British political leaders are only adapting slowly. In formal terms (Greer and Trench 2008), the devolution legislation is clear that EU matters are for the UK, and if a devolved government breaches EU law it pays the fines (though if the UK is sued by the Commission for a devolved infraction, the damages, known as *Francovich* damages after an ECJ case, would be paid by the UK and not all officials were clear that the UK could claw it back from devolved budgets) (Trench 2007). This has already twice led the UK government to deter devolved governments from non-health policies that in its (rather narrow) interpretation would leave it open to challenges whose costs, in case of defeat, it would extract from their budgets. The legislation and the White Papers surrounding the birth of the devolved bodies are also clear that the UK should consult the devolved administrations and take their views into account (Jeffery and Palmer 2007).

The ambiguity worked well for the first decade of devolution. Regardless of whether they invented the model or learned, the officials responsible for the UK, Scotland and Wales in Brussels developed what might be the EU's most successful model of regional influence – a relative score, given that it means only that there was less complaint than from most other ambitious regions about their member states. Northern Ireland, Scotland and Wales operated, on one hand, as lobbies: Scotland and Wales both have large offices at the Rond-Point Schumann, the symbolic centre of the EU, and they are active in pan-EU regional groupings. But the devolved governments also worked through the UK: being able to co-ordinate their own lobbying with the power and resources of a major EU member state gave them the best of both worlds.

Such an ability to work together depends on goodwill. Goodwill is not always a satisfactory basis for government. There are three basic problems with the UK approach. First, the UK government is dominant. That might not sit well in case of divergence or even fit with Scotland's current self-projection. Second, quite predictably, the big organizations of Whitehall could not be bothered to regularly integrate their work with Scotland. Whitehall officials do not need to be very busy or defensive to forget about Scotland. That is a feature of organizational life. But there is a third and bigger problem: the UK applies standard interdepartmental dispute resolution mechanisms to intergovernmental disputes. But administrative procedure is unlikely to produce agreement when the disagreement is political.

Departmental

[The question is] how do we prioritise what people do to ensure inputting and influencing the right ways. Rather than ad hoc, with people going to meetings because they are interested as a personal project on the side. Also, the budgets are tight. I think the strategy of a small central unit, essentially managing, helping and consulting to the policy leads for European business is the right strategy. I am not sure I see a better way, really.

(UK official)

The departmental level, of course, is where much EU health policy is actually made, but it is also where health policymakers are most likely to find themselves in a ghetto, talking about public health advertising campaigns while finance and industry departments decide whether health should be in the Services Directive. The UK does benefit from generalism and a longstanding civil service habit of distributing information widely as well as the international travels of its top officials. This means that it is more able to co-ordinate at the lower levels; the network properties of its civil service and the relatively high rank of the Department of Health among ministries mean that co-ordination can often work to the benefit of the health sector. The UK makes it very hard for departments to 'hide', but that is not a problem when the DH is often able to win in intragovernmental conflict.

Despite the mainstreaming efforts, at most of the higher-level policy events, it is a member of the International Division that turns up with perhaps a few others. Given that the DH, like its equivalents, lacks what my French interviewee called a 'European culture', mainstreaming EU health policy is still a pending assignment for the UK.

It is at the departmental level that the devolved health ministries tend to fall out of sight. Health ministries tend to be small relative to their health systems, and in a small health system such as that of Northern Ireland or Wales, it means that only small fractions of a small number of people can be dedicated to EU health issues. It is also easy for individuals' international activities, rightly or wrongly, to stand in for organized attention to the issue. Asking devolved policymakers who was responsible for EU affairs tends to produce a mixture of people with EU policy in their job description and people dotted around the health departments who do things with a European aspect that might have little or nothing to do with the EU. The result is that the devolved health departments have quite sensibly relied on the UK Department of Health. It is not so much a delegation of devolved departmental roles to the DH as a fiduciary relationship: the devolved departments have usually not taken up opportunities to follow EU issues closely and assume that the UK DH can defend their interests on most issues. Experts based on devolved systems do attend EU events, but that is generally because they are networked directly with the DH (this is especially common with the high-status Scottish medical academics). Only from mid-2008 did a devolved office head in Brussels say that EU health was a coming issue – and that from the head of the most attuned office, the Welsh.

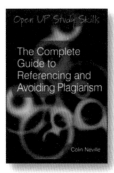
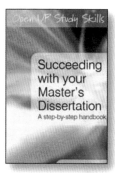

McGraw-Hill Higher Education

OPEN UNIVERSITY PRESS
McGraw - Hill Education

cipd

Examination Copy Feedback

Thank you for considering our books for your teaching.

We value your feedback. Please let us know whether or not the book is suitable for your module.

If you have received a McGraw-Hill book, please visit:
www.mcgraw-hill.co.uk/response

If you have received an Open University Press book, please visit: www.openup.co.uk/response

If you have received a CIPD book, please visit:
www.mcgraw-hill.co.uk/cipdfeedback

If you require supplements to support your McGraw-Hill textbook, please contact your local academic rep: www.mcgraw-hill.co.uk/he/rep

ISBN-13: 978-007711916-4
ISBN-10: 007711916-9

9 780077 119164

Deliberative

If the UK and France are the paragons of a strategic, co-ordinated and nimble approach at the diplomatic and departmental levels, it is the UK and Germany that stand out as effective at the deliberative level. That is partly down to the efforts of the Department of Health itself to engage with Brussels debates, as well as its ability to field very effective officials in EU policy debates.

But it is also down to the many different channels by which the UK lobbies in the EU health policy sector. Several interviewees commented on the paradox that the UK is both a famously 'Eurosceptic' country and a bed of people who operate very successfully in EU politics.[4] UK lobbyists and citizens are ubiquitous in the EU, including a few who work for organizations in Brussels that have no UK members or relevance. Even more than Germans, it is very easy to find influential people in EU health debates who are based in or come from the UK.

One relationship is particularly interesting. The inevitably unstable relationship between the NHS and the Department of Health influences what is going on here. The NHS, especially in England, is public sector, and might in principle expect the Department of Health to just speak for it. But instead, the NHS organizations themselves have organized lobbies to speak for themselves in Brussels with the full support of the Department of Health. German insurance funds can go ahead and lobby in Brussels if they want to, but it might be more of a surprise to see NHS organizations doing it, given that they are quite literally the property of the various UK governments.

NHS lobbying started with a number of ill-assorted NHS units that opted to hire Brussels officers, usually housed in their regional lobby office in Brussels (Greer 2006a). Most were regions, such as the West Midlands, Northwest and Greater London, but a few individual local organizations also hired part-time EU policy officers (including the Hove Primary Care Trust). I interviewed each one, and in each case the model was similar despite considerable variation in the specifics. A single entrepreneur, usually a senior public health officer, would become interested in EU affairs and decide that it was a strategic issue for the NHS as a whole. This person would persuade a number of organizations in the region to fund an officer, who would then spend quite a lot of time lobbying backwards, demonstrating the relevance of the EU and the good value of the office with mechanisms such as newsletters and personal briefings. After a while the unstable and small-scale nature of this activity and entrepreneurship by groups such as the Nuffield Trust persuaded the organization that represents NHS organizations' management, the NHS Confederation, to open a Brussels office to speak on behalf of the NHS systems as a whole, paid for out of contributions from across all four systems. The Department of Health remained in the background: officials told me explicitly that the UK government believed that the NHS should be more independent and that there was no guarantee that NHS managers would always agree with the government on EU policy (Greer and Rauscher 2008).

CONCLUSION: INFORMED, CO-ORDINATED, NIMBLE?

> France and the UK have the same basic approach. When France and the UK agree on an issue (which is not often) we succeed because we can enter into and organize movement. That was the case with the Services Directive.
>
> (French official)

The UK, in the early twenty-first century, is probably the 'best' big EU member state. It is informed and active across the deliberative, departmental and diplomatic levels. That is partly because the EU model that it generalized to health works well, and partly because the same unitary culture that makes Europeanization disagreeable for many in British politics also makes it an effective actor in Brussels.

But that success is, like every EU health model, due to the factors that shape the overall approach of the UK. Constitutions, changes in public administration and the health ministry, rather than adaptation to the demands of EU politics, shape what member states do and the UK is no exception. Its unitary model is in large part a souvenir of the days when it was a union state with a Whitehall civil service. But the UK has evolved appreciably from that, with devolution and the ongoing transformation of its civil service. The most visible disjunction is in the relative absence of the devolved health departments at the departmental level, where they let the DH do the work for them. It remains to be seen whether this works when current nebulous debates turn into firmer legal obligations with, possibly, an English tint. The latent disjunctions are between a system premised on hierarchy and comity, and politics that produce the reverse. There is no particular reason to expect that EU health policy will be the site of an intergovernmental battle in the UK, but there is no reason not to expect it (Greer and Trench 2008). Until the UK stabilizes its intergovernmental relations, and develops civil service and political cultures adapted to devolution, there will be adequate tinder for an intergovernmental conflagration, and health politics in the UK tend to be rather hot.

The quality and flexibility of UK engagement in Brussels is due not only to the functionality of the DH, but also to the activity and ubiquity of people based in or from the UK. That particularly matters at the deliberative level. Their diversity probably also helps promote the autonomy of health policy. On the diplomatic and departmental levels, for example, the UK DH is publicly calm about most EU issues, including sensitive ones such as public procurement. Despite the proclaimed internationalism of Plaid Cymru and (especially) the SNP, there is not much devolved attention going to the question of how to avoid begin caught in interpretations of EU law developed for and by the English. But the many lobbies from the UK, including the four-system NHS Confederation, the Royal Colleges and the many UK policy entrepreneurs working in Brussels, bring these issues up at times when the DH is actually focusing on the benefits of the EU policies.

NOTES

1   To understand the UK NHS system, two books are crucial: Ham (2004) and Klein (2006).
2   Already, the main judgment in which the UK's Competition Commission set out the application of EU law to competition among providers in the UK health system (by a nursing home company complaining that the local health services 'abused a dominant position'), came not from England but from a case in Northern Ireland. *BetterCare Group Ltd / North & West Belfast Health & Social Services Trust* no. CA98/09/2003.
3   According to one Cabinet Secretary (the head of the Home Civil Service), writing in 1950, the

> system of recruitment provided a great bond of unity between the staffs in the different Departments; the bond of having entered by the same gate and being of the same vintage, or perhaps a year more or less in bottle than Smith of the Department across the road.
>
> (Bridges 1950)

4   The term 'Eurosceptic' is a euphemism. Most declared 'Eurosceptics' are not sceptical; they are anti-EU. For the relatively high (though by no means unique) level of opposition to the EU, see Eurobarometer's quarterly reports. In the spring of 2008, the UK was tied with Austria

and Latvia as the member state with the smallest percentage of the population that thought the 'European Union conjure[s] up a very positive [or] fairly positive . . . image' (28%). The EU average was 44% and the equivalent number for Germany was 48%, for France 44% and for Spain 59%. Amusingly, the Republic of Ireland had the second highest positive response, with 65% (Eurobarometer 2008).

10

SPAIN

Spain, we might say, combines a French attitude to public administration with a level of territorial diversity more like that of the UK,
and produces the highest level of fragmentation of our four countries. Spain decentralized a French-style Jacobin state by carving out
areas – of policy, of law, of money and of administrative resources –
for the autonomous communities (Solé-Tura 1986). The state
remained intact but with fewer powers, responsibilities and resources.
In health, this meant a lengthy process, spread over approximately
1979–2000, during which the autonomous communities took over
responsibility for health services and public health such as it is. The
Jacobin state remains, with many centralist tendencies, but it lacks
powers to do much of what it might expect to do. The other side of
the coin, historically, is the mobilization of stateless nations and
some strong regions: Catalonia and the Basque Country, pre-
eminently, but also Galicia and the distinctive but non-nationalist
Andalucia and Valencia. Two centuries of Spanish history have been
about the state's efforts to assimilate them and their efforts to gain
autonomy or independence. The democratic constitution of 1979 did
much to resolve the tension with autonomy for regional governments, but the tradition and fact of regional-central contention is
still very important. Spanish intergovernmental relations have been
zero-sum and contentious; Catalonia, the Basque Country and some
other autonomous communities 'won' powers from the central state
in 20 years of administrative struggle.

The history of Spanish intergovernmental relations since 1979 has
been one of coping with these tensions, initially with an emphasis on
combat and disharmony, and more recently to an emphasis on
'building in' the autonomous communities. At each step the process

has been highly political, with the partisan complexions of different governments crucial to understanding their approach to inter-governmental relations. But it has also been the clearest case of relatively apolitical learning of our four countries; Spanish governments have found that policymaking and implementation in health and EU politics demand a level of co-ordination if they are all to avoid being losers.

It takes place against a backdrop of historic Spanish enthusiasm for 'Europe' in the abstract and often as a synonym of modernization and democratization. This is part of a revealing Spanish relationship with very deep roots and significance (Kamen 2007) but also meant that Spanish political elites very concretely saw joining the EU as a transition 'from ostracism to modernity' (MacLennan 2004). In health, European integration was long particularly interesting to public health advocates, who are historically weak in Spain (Fundación de Ciencias de la Salud 1997). Spanish attitudes are not simple.[1] Interviewees from Spain commented on the Spanish willingness to just accept and go along with EU policies rather than reflect on them, but they, others and some academic literature also point out the nationalist threads in Spanish thought about Europe, and Spain's fierce negotiations in the EU when its interests are threatened (Balfour and Quiroga 2007: 161–196; Díez Medrano 2000). Spain has the intellectual and political resources to pursue its interests in Brussels, but on most issues in health its governments have not defined an interest, or have defined it with more of an eye on their domestic issues than on what works in EU politics.

SYSTEM AND STAKES

The Spanish health care system is a web of 17 health care systems run by its powerful regional governments, which are known as 'autonomous communities'. As in the UK, there is relatively little interpenetration between the central state and the regional health systems. The legal framework set by the state is broad and permits substantial variation, although the Spanish system is more comprehensible and makes clear statements of goals. The financial framework separates the central state from health policy by making block grants to regional governments which they are then free to allocate as they choose (rather than making funding contingent on particular health policies).

This decentralization, while in its details is a legacy of the particular sequence of events in Spanish democratic politics, also reflects the nature and importance of territorial politics in Spain. Spain has a long history of failure to integrate big stateless nations (especially Catalonia and the Basque Country) that muster many kinds of political power, from money to votes to the threat of violence. Integrating them non-violently was a key task of politicians during its democratic transition. The solution, the system of autonomous communities, gave democratic voice to the aspirations of nationalist and autonomist political forces, and gave considerable policy power to the new regional governments. They proceeded to lobby for more power, as regional governments tend to do, while other Spanish politicians generalized the model across the rest of the country. The result is a member state that is still diverse, but whose diversity is represented by, and has been increased by, its powerful level of regional government (Aja 1999; Greer 2007b; Subirats 2006).

System

Spain is divided into 17 regions, each with considerable autonomy in health policy and relatively stable funding entrenched in a law. They vary considerably as a function of the chronology of Spanish politics: the first autonomous communities took over health care and established distinctive models years before the central state passed the 1983 basic law setting out norms for the health system (and codifying, if not actually creating, universal coverage). As a result, there are a variety of distinctive Spanish health care models, with Madrid, Catalonia, Valencia, the Basque Country, Navarre and Andalucia particularly likely to develop different and perhaps innovative policies (Gallego et al. 2002, 2003; Subirats and Gallego 2002).

   Despite these variations, the basic Spanish model of health care is a national health care model in which the autonomous communities finance health care out of a large block budget fixed as a percentage of income. They provide services directly, although there is always a tendency for the system to become a residual one; many of the more elite occupations and employees of the biggest firms, including many health system workers, politicians and civil servants, belong to effectively private mutual societies that fund their health care. The autonomous communities vary in the extent of this residualism, with some (such as Madrid) relying heavily on the mutuals and decreasing funding to the public system. They also vary in the extent and nature of private and non-profit provision to the public sector, with Catalonia noteworthy for its contracts with municipal and non-profit hospitals for a large part of its care and the right-wing show-case Madrid also notable for its use of PFIs and private providers. The system is an overall success (Rico Gómez et al. 2007).

Stakes

The 'Spanish case' (as a German interviewee called it) is the most obvious case of patient mobility in Europe: British and (some) German retirees living on the Spanish coasts. This is probably the place in Europe where the most difficult interactions between EU health law and real humans take place (Ackers and Dwyer 2002; King et al. 2000; Rosenmöller and Lluch 2006). The basic issue is that the Spanish coasts host many retirees who buy property, do not learn Spanish, and are very poorly integrated with Spanish society. This can rapidly turn into sad situations; a common one is when a couple moves to Spain, one person becomes dependent or dies, and an elderly partner with neither language nor legal skills is obliged to master Spanish social welfare provision. The Spanish, meanwhile, find their social welfare infrastructure, which was built for (very different) Spanish family patterns, is inadequate for caring for these citizens. Add in the effects of seasonal influxes of tourists, and the result is a serious change in patterns of health resource use and a large number of monoglot patients who are difficult to treat (whether confused elderly people or drugged nightclubbers). Putting aside the human problems, this is costly and potentially asks the Spanish not only to provide treatment that will be uncertainly recompensed later, but also to make serious changes to service provision and planning. Social security law helps, but not fully; problems arise whether retirees transfer benefits to Spain or not. But many people just go to Spain, and only later realize the complexity of getting treatment.

Like the UK, Spain also has the problem that its system for pricing services is weak; because their systems did not need or use as many transactions, the prices that facilities charged non-citizens or that were used in internal transactions often bore little resemblance to real costs. Ignoring this, the Court has effectively imposed the obligation (in *Watts*) to develop internal pricing not because that is more efficient, but because there is no other way to charge patients under EU law. It is a regulatory compliance cost and is emblematic of the gap between simple judicial ideas and health systems' operations.

Decentralization means that different Spanish systems have slightly different exposures to EU legal risk. They vary in the extent, type and sophistication of their contracting for provision and support services, as well as the subsidies granted to various public providers. So, for example, competition law, public procurement and state aids all pose potential problems, especially in the systems such as Madrid that contract out major parts of the health care system or systems such as that of Catalonia which combine public commissioning, a public provider that receives direct subsidies for its facilities as well as contracts, and private providers, often with municipal government support, that also receive subsidies as well as contracts (Fernández Farreres 2006).

The chance of a challenge is increased by interaction between EU law and the small-scale politics of Spanish health care is also murky. One major case, *FENIN*, is not Spanish by accident; it was caused by public sector organizations delaying payment (and then arguing, faced with an EU challenge, that they were exempt as public sector organizations). Delayed payments are a relatively common practice in the Spanish public sector, and it is not surprising that it was a delayed payment that led the vendors' association to sue. Local webs of complicity in a given autonomous community can damp down conflict and allow practices that are not really legal to go on, but the behaviour they sustain can collapse if somebody decides to challenge them.

The disjunction between regional health policy autonomy and areas of unified public law creates the same problem that the UK might encounter – precedents created by one system spilling over. Spain has a unified legal system, with most commercial and contract law firmly in the hands of the central state's judiciary despite areas of law that vary between regional governments (such as state aids law) (Fernández Farreres 2006). So it is possible that a case quite specific to a single system will produce interpretations of EU law that are extended to other Spanish systems that have slightly different problems but end up under the same decisions.

Constitutionally, Spain also faces the risk that EU health policies will reduce regional autonomy by the back door. The central state has the competency for EU relations, but the autonomous communities have enormous responsibilities for health care. It is the autonomous communities that suffer should EU law reduce the autonomy of health care decision-makers. And as usual, in so far as any part of the Spanish state has input into those decisions, it is the central state. As a Catalan nationalist parliamentarian once told me of his party's aspirations for a 'Europe of the Regions': 'What we didn't see was just how much juridical statehood mattered' (Greer 2007b: 31).

EXPLAINING SPAIN'S EU HEALTH POLICY

Spanish EU health policy is harder to characterize than that of France, Germany and the UK because it is less active at every level.[2] Two interviewees from other countries went out of their way to note that they had never seen a single proposal from Spanish representatives in departmental-level gatherings, and several others quizzed me about Spanish ideas and policies. People might puzzle out the tactics or ultimate intentions of the UK or France, but nobody suggested their positions were simply incoherent. Spain stands in for the many EU countries that have very little influence on European Union health policy: it is, over and over again, a policy-taker rather than a policymaker. Its public administration and the division of responsibilities in its health care system explain why. But the division of responsibilities also means that it sheds light on, and contains some useful lessons for, states that are attempting to fit together regional, member state, and EU political arenas.

Constitution

Arguably one of the most important themes of Spanish constitutional politics has been the articulation between the central state, which often had centralizing nation-building and state-building ambitions, and the stateless nations of Catalonia, the Basque Country and Galicia, as well as the localisms of various intensity that came from the same failure of the centralizing state to repress them in the way France successfully did. Failure to balance territorial diversity was at the root of a series of the worst episodes in Spanish modern history, and creating a stable territorial settlement by decentralizing power to autonomous communities was a preoccupation of the politicians who created democratic Spain in the late 1970s and their successors. In health, the development of the 'state of the autonomies' has led to the central government almost completely decoupling itself from the organization and finance of health care services. Fixed formulas set in law determine the financing of regional governments, occasionally supplemented by large bailouts of the autonomous communities. There is a 'basic law' of 1986 structuring the system, and obliging autonomous communities to adhere to certain standards, but their requirements are mostly beneath the level of existing regional government activity.

Spanish intergovernmental relations have been in flux because its constitutional politics have been in flux, so some political history is necessary. A key moment in Spanish autonomous history was the dependence of the minority Partido Popular (PP) government led by José Maria Aznar government on the votes of nationalist and other small parties between 1996 and 2000. Part of their price was the creation of a mechanism that would allow them to more effectively engage in central state policies; this included 'sectoral' or 'interterritorial' councils that would improve information sharing and establish shared decision-making between the autonomous communities and the central state. The Aznar government's absolute majority in the 2000 election muddied the water substantially. The often poisonous conflicts between Madrid and the Catalan and Basque political leadership overshadowed the low-level institutionalization of the councils. It also limited their high-level effectiveness because it meant that there were not many politicians who were willing to accept influence from other governments. Between 2000 and 2004 it required an optimist to focus on the institutionalization and ignore the conflicts.

The election of the minority Zapatero government in 2004, with much of its small plurality from Catalan votes, and coming after the victory of a Socialist-led coalition in Catalonia, marked a major change in Madrid's strategy and in Spanish intergovernmental relations. Zapatero's Socialist party, the PSOE, is the strongest statewide party; the Popular party, its main Spanish opposition, is weak in the Basque Country and (especially) Catalonia. This enabled Zapatero's broad shift in intergovernmental relations. Aznar's government, and the Popular party, often ran *against* 'the nationalists' (as they refer to the Catalan, Basque and smaller nationalist parties). By contrast, the Socialists' obvious strategy is to develop a web of shared interests with a variety of small parties so that they will have a range of supporters in the Spanish parliament as well as an electoral base across the country. Add in the merits of defusing conflict – above all in the Basque Country – and there is a compelling case for Socialist governments to make intergovernmental relations less political and more co-ordinated.

The Socialist approach to intergovernmental relations involved a number of related fronts. The most public and contested was the development of new Statutes of Autonomy for various autonomous communities. This allowed the Socialists to negotiate and grant expanded powers for the autonomous communities without opening

up the politically dangerous topic of constitutional reform. The statutes sometimes disappointed: Catalonia got significantly less than it
requested while the Basque Country proved intractable. But they
expanded autonomous community power and might have closed the
opportunity for further reform on that 'high politics' level.

Public administration

On paper, Spain is hierarchical and French. Like France, Spain has a
tradition of ministerial advisers with key roles at the top of the
formal civil service hierarchy; while officials interact with ministers
in all the systems, the minister's advisers play a key role in formulating the ministerial agenda. It also has a tradition of political
appointment of top bureaucrats that goes beyond the political
appointees in French and German civil service posts. Several levels
down into the ministry, there are still political appointees, many of
them established figures from the policy community (such as academics specializing in various areas of health policy and public
health). If political appointees come from within the sector, this ties
the public administration close to its sector, although they need not.
At one point the Ministry of Health and Consumption (MSC) had a
Director General for Public Health who was actually qualified in
veterinary medicine, not human or public health medicine (and the
EU health specialist at another time was trained in Arab language
and culture). The problem is that, in practice, political appointment
produces turnover and, in lightly staffed areas such as EU health
policy, it means that any institutional memory is lodged so far down
the hierarchy as to have little influence over policy.

Political appointment and consequent turnover produce immediate, notable effects. One former official responsible for EU affairs in
the MSC pointed out the importance of networks. Key officials,
including the UK and German civil servants, would travel to Brussels
the night before major meetings, have dinner, and discuss their goals
and work through issues. It did not necessarily decide the outcome
of the meeting, but it would certainly influence it. 'If you take the
first flight from Madrid, you miss that. It means that you don't know
what the others are doing and don't understand how to influence it.
Spanish people never seem to do that'.

At the same time, Spain has not seen much civil service reform
(Gallego 2003), and so the permanent civil servants are often chosen
by rigid processes that discourage corruption but do not necessarily
fit person and job effectively. Toward the top, Spain, like France, has

corps (*cuerpos*) of civil servants chosen by examination who are then eligible for certain jobs. The MSC does not have such a *cuerpo* of its own, which is one of many markers of its weakness. It has many doctors (who, like NHS managers in the UK, have experience of health and health systems but might not understand the state structure well) and is partially colonized by the legally trained TACs (administrative technicians of the state). TACs share an outlook, and form a network across the spending ministries of the government, but are a thin basis on which to expect generalism and cost-reducing information networks, let alone much engagement in EU health politics.

Health ministry

The ministry used to have direct responsibility for providing health services for most of Spain. Now it runs essentially nothing, and its plans for cohesion and co-ordination of services are merely advisory. This poses a major strategic challenge for the ministry, and leads many outsiders (especially Catalans) to ask what its thousands of employees are doing all day. Interviewees from the autonomous communities tend to see its usefulness as confined to international relations (such as tracking people with infectious diseases; 'We cannot call a hospital in Italy to trace a patient, but the state can', explained one Catalan official in 2007).

Since the handover of the last major health care systems to the autonomous communities, there has been a level of legal and administrative activity, including a law of Cohesion and Quality (2003) that purports to structure the 'National Health System' and a series of integrated plans for various diseases that have neither coercive force nor money behind them. Cohesion is the banner for an effort to unify and guarantee standards through a contentious and still largely undefined mix of consensual and imposed standards. It might lead to nothing at all; that will depend on the political skills and agendas in Madrid and the autonomous communities.

The year 2008 marked a further reduction in the power of the ministry. The Zapatero government removed as much of the MSC's research capacity as it could in order to build up a new department responsible for research and higher education. This influenced some aspects of health system governance, because the Instituto Carlos III that provides information for health systems became a joint venture of the two ministries. More important, it reduced the small power base of the ministry yet further. Ministries' power comes from laws, money and resources (such as skilled staff); any reduction in them reduces the ability of the ministry to shape agendas and decisions in interministerial co-ordination or develop EU policy proposals and responses. After the departmental reorganization, the MSC had still less power. This is not a promising base from which to develop ideas for the EU agenda or make health concerns important in formulating overall Spanish approaches to the EU.

SPAIN'S EU MODEL IN HEALTH

Spain sounds much like our other countries on paper, but it has the classic characteristic of a state with poorly organized EU relations: it is strongest at the diplomatic level. The diplomatic level is, of course, where adaptation to the EU is most coercive (there has to be a Permanent Representation), where the spotlight of high-level political attention is most important, and where knowledge of policy and future policy options tends to be least important. Fortunately for Spain, it is also a level where it is powerful due to distortions in the weighted voting of the Council that give it and Poland almost as many votes as much larger France, Germany, Italy and the UK. Perhaps Spanish weakness at all but the diplomatic level explains part of the ferocity with which it has defended its overrepresentation in Council voting.

The diplomatic focus tends to mean that Spain does not shape debates, but rather negotiates hard at the end. In addition, Spain has had difficulty settling the relationship between its autonomous communities and the central state in EU policy as well as other areas. The prominence of the EU in Spanish politics, and the autonomous communities' sense that they were (like their German counterparts) losing a role to Brussels and lacked a voice in Brussels, led to a long series of negotiations and modifications that try to build the autonomous communities into Spanish EU policy as well as autonomous community efforts to address Brussels directly.

Diplomatic

In theory, the MSC is responsible for developing EU policy ideas and conducting impact assessment. It then works with the Secretariat of State for European Affairs (SEAE), which is the central co-ordinating unit. The SEAE, like the French SGAE, has varied in its official status (the rank of its political and civil service heads, and its relationship with the ministry of foreign affairs). Unlike the SGAE, it has not been able to monopolize Spain's formal EU policies in the same way; while the Spanish central government is quite hier-archical, it has turned out to be difficult to instil a bureaucratic culture of information sharing. It also has the problem that as part of the central state it is a long distance from the autonomous com-munities, which are responsible for most Spanish health policy, and the long tradition of central-regional suspicion maintains much of that distance.

The result is that the SEAE, supposedly the key co-ordinator, is an 'arena' for debates over EU policy more than a monopolist of EU policymaking (Molina Álvarez de Cienfuegos 2001: 163). This can mean the most intense forms of interdepartmental, intragovernmen-tal conflict. In such conflict, the MSC, as a weak ministry, is unlikely to win. That is the case even when the autonomous communities – which share its interests in expanded welfare provision – agree with it and lobby for its same causes.

In Brussels, the Spanish permanent representation fulfils the same tasks as the other permanent representations, with dossiers on health typically prepared by the Ministry of Health and routed through the SEAE. Given that Spanish co-ordination tends to happen at the very top, and is often done by the diplomats of the Ministry of Foreign Affairs, technical and lower priority issues often go unexamined until the last minute, if even then. This shows in relatively vague instructions for Spanish officials at lower-level events, occasional last-minute decisions by the centre, and technical problems. On major issues, such as the patient mobility legislation, the problem is not so great because there had been discussion for years, as Spanish representatives pointed out. Nevertheless other member state repre-sentatives were confused by Spanish stances in the Council working groups that were understandable as policy but appeared to contra-vene key ECJ rulings, and a number of interviewees from Spain and other countries suggested that the Permanent Representation, MSC and political advisers to the government were working at cross purposes.

Naturally, such an arrangement at the centre of government is a poor fit with autonomous communities that often see their own international projection as an end in itself. Even if Andalucian health policy is not very distinctive, it is important for Andalucia that its health policy have some representation in Brussels. The Basque Country and Catalonia are particularly emphatic: like Scotland, they see international activity ('projection') as an end in itself and an affirmation of their nationality (Urgell 2003). And given that Spain lacks German imperatives to co-ordination and consensus, the Spanish regions and government are free to block and counteract each other.

The result has been poor co-ordination, exacerbated by the central state's own tendencies to fragmentation and tardiness. Region–state tension increased policy and implementation problems for the state, and regional governments were frustrated by their inability to influence the Spanish vote in the Council meetings that decided so many important policies. The solution was a quasi-German innovation: 'sectoral councils' in which the autonomous communities and central state meet to discuss and co-ordinate policies. The health council is known as the 'interterritorial council' and the EU affairs council, which processes all information about the EU and distributes it to the appropriate regional departments, is called CARCE (Conference for Matters Related to the European Communities). The Ministry of Public Administrations organizes and attends all the councils but the interterritorial (health) council.

Councils are a dependent variable more than an independent one. Between 2000 and 2008, the best that could be pointed out was that the councils, when not humbly doing their job, were sometimes seen as the appropriate forum for arguments. The Councils have agreed agendas and the Madrid government must inform autonomous communities of major issues. While the Spanish councils for health (focused on co-ordinating life and death issues like transplant organs) and Europe work well by Spanish standards, information, agendas and initiatives are still weapons in them, and all the players are quite capable failure to co-ordinate. As one interviewee explained: 'They are ministers, and they are all free to go home and do what they like'.

In EU health policy formulation, the changes with the Zapatero government were less visible but shaped by their place in the new overall Socialist approach to intergovernmental relations, and the longstanding interest many Spanish thinkers had for German practices. The most dramatic change was opening up the Council itself to the autonomous communities. The autonomous communities can send delegates to four councils including the Health Council, where they may speak, in agreement with the Spanish position. This ability to speak in the Council is dramatic by the standards of EU policy-making (even if most citizens would probably find the Council rather dull) and autonomous community governments' press offices will sometimes make a big play of it. Regions can have representatives in comitology (largely outside health), which might be more important because of their well-documented autonomy. The policy is what matters, and a regional government of any country that is representing a position it dislikes is nothing more than an unusual sort of diplomat.

The policies in health and social policy are subject to the increasingly co-ordinated policy process developed by the Zapatero government. In it, there is an extensive agenda of issues that the councils discuss, with a substantial flow of paper between them and a much higher level of information exchange than took place under Aznar (Conferencia para asuntos relacionados con las Comunidades Europeas 2006). The Councils should, in principle, agree positions by majority vote, but in practice they work best when there is agreement, or a majority of autonomous communities with a shared position that they can negotiate with the central government. The central government's freedom is mostly a function of the level of autonomous community diversity, or disengagement. Given the relatively low salience of EU health policy in Spain, and the broad ideological congruence between governments on issues such as the Services Directive, there has not been too much tension here.

Departmental

At the departmental level Spain is also weak. This is in large part a function of its structure: the MSC is the weakest health ministry of our four because it lacks power over health systems within Spain. The ministry, like its peer departments, conducts lower-level EU operations more or less on its own. That means it is the key actor in the OMC, High Level Group and other forums. As with the other countries, there is a theoretical need for the centre to monitor potential cross-departmental conflicts, but such everyday, active co-ordination is rare.

Within the MSC, international affairs suffers from a basic problem: it is a subordinate function of the subsecretary of the department, a post that is responsible more for departmental management than for policy. The person responsible for EU matters is relatively low level (contrary to what might be expected, the lack of alternative policy areas has not made the MSC focus more on international health policy issues). That is not necessarily a problem; no member state posts top-level civil servants to the international division of a health ministry. The Spanish problem, interviewees inside and outside the ministry argued, is that the low status of the person comes with and reinforces a low status attributed to the issue of EU health policy. At the Permanent Representation, meanwhile, there are also problems of ensuring administrative continuity between staff; short overlap times make it difficult to maintain institutional memory.

The autonomous communities, like the German Länder, might multiply the departmental-level representation by backing up the ministry or at least attending. They all have Brussels offices, and since EPSCO is one in which they play a role, they follow EU health policy. A seemingly small decision limits their engagement; they decided to rotate topics rather than follow the German or Italian model and choose which government would lead among them on a given policy area. This can mean that the importance of the issue and the capacity (or interest) of the leading autonomous community can be misaligned. It also means, given the small numbers of people involved, that credibility, networks and institutional memory are harmed during the handovers between autonomous communities. The departmental level is one on which personal credibility, preparation and assiduity matter greatly. The MSC has difficulty delivering that, and the organization of regional health ministries' engagement does not help them fill in the gap.

In other words, the departmental level of Spanish EU policy is weak. The MSC is weak, and this spills over into its ability to operate EU policies, and it shares some of the problems of Spanish public administration, such as hierarchy and a relatively high degree of political appointment. The regional health departments are engaged, but their engagement has not solidified into the kind of effective backup, or at least specific network, that Germany enjoys. Departmental-level weakness can and in many countries does exist in symbiosis with effectiveness at the diplomatic level. Member states, unlike lobbies, can rescue a lost cause with effective negotiating at the end, even if all the Spanish can often get is a delay in implementation of EU legislation. But they also have to operate very defensively and in a focused manner if they have not set the agenda. In the worst case scenario, they will be seeking exemptions and transition periods for EU policies influenced, if influenced by any member state, by very different countries such as France, Germany and the UK.

Deliberative

It is here that decentralization helps Spain (and, still more, Italy). The activities of the regions mean that they sometimes participate in the informal debates that take before legislation is published. That is the good news; the Spanish regions are sometimes to be found moving debates in which the state is absent. But it is from a low base of deliberative participation; not all the Spanish regions are engaged or effective. The Spanish state, which participates rather minimally in departmental-level forums such as the High Level Group, rarely engages at the deliberative level of policy.

Beyond that, there is not much more good news. Spain is relatively inactive: a low rate of affiliation to EU-level groups and participation in forums such as consultations or the Platform, relatively small numbers of Spanish citizens in key jobs among interest groups, and near invisibility of Spanish officials or civil servants at meetings and debates. Formal gatherings like the Council working groups afford Spain a platform to raise its (serious) issues, above all the consequences of patient mobility, but its arguments are dominated by complaint about the 'Spanish case' of massive foreign patient presence. In lobbies, the 2008 breakup of the doctors' peak lobby CPME was emblematic of the Spanish difficulty lobbying; Spanish discontent with the perceived northern bias of the lobby reflected decades of more effective lobbying and alliance-building within the organization by 'northerners'. Spain's health care system lacks a culture of lobbying, and that includes Brussels lobbying.

CONCLUSION: INFORMED, CO-ORDINATED, NIMBLE?

Spain's is a happy story from some points of view, including because it teaches us about concrete techniques and political approaches that can improve even very bad intergovernmental relations. There is more that can be done; the interterritorial councils are still not built on a platform of formal equality between governments, and observers in some autonomous communities are keen to point out the formal and informal ways that the central government can shape the outcomes. Likewise, there is more scope for political change in Spain than in Germany or France. A dramatic election result in the central government, or a number of autonomous communities, could still put the newly constructed system of intergovernmental relations under pressure. But the growing institutionalization of EU relations also means that the networks and soft skills, and activity, of the more prominent autonomous communities (Andalucia, the Basque Country, Catalonia and Valencia), make Spain a more active country in EU health politics than it would otherwise be.

On the other hand, Spain does not shape EU health debates.

Spanish EU policy historically shows that a determined and well-organized diplomatic-level effort on salient issues (such as EU funding) can work very well, but it is not necessarily shaping the debate. Its informal and (still) formal fragmentation means that in Brussels the Spanish often work at cross purposes. It probably reinforces the noted Spanish tendency to reactiveness; in any list of major EU countries, Spain is far behind the others in its ability to identify and engage with emerging policy issues, and while it can formulate a line, it is often a line hierarchically imposed by Madrid without enough input from the rest of the government, the Permanent Representation, subject specialists or autonomous communities.

Spain looks relatively good compared to some of its peers, such as Italy, because Spain is very good at pursuing a few policy objectives, not many of which touch on health. They are, typically, structural funds, fisheries, certain agricultural subsidies (often still picking apart deals sealed just before Spanish accession) and permission to delay implementation of EU laws. But that is often a result of, first, the intensity of Spanish interests in fish, regional development and such like, and second, of the focus of the Spanish EU bureaucracy on those topics. The effectiveness does not spill outside the areas of constant political attention, and is still mostly at high-level negotiation stages, not earlier stages of policy influence when governments can exert softer forms of power if they know what they want. That is exactly why Spain is best at the diplomatic level, and that also suggests why the diplomatic level is the place where we see the least variation in states' adaptation to, or influence in, EU politics.

NOTES

1 Despite some symbolism: Spain was the first member state to ratify the treaty establishing a constitution, and for a few months it was easy to buy souvenirs and shirts around Madrid reading 'Los Primeros con Europa'.
2 Also it enjoys a smaller academic literature. Apart from the recent and excellent Morata and Mateo (2007), the two principal works are Closa (2001) and Closa and Heywood (2004).

11

CONCLUSION

The European Union is a principal strategic challenge for EU health systems today. That does not mean it is necessarily a problem, or that it will do much good, or that it will inflict drastic costs on the health care systems of Europe. It is simply indeterminate, and the challenge is to understand and do something about it.

First, it is possible to go through every policy issue listed in Chapter 3 and identify ways that it can be made relatively unimportant; compliance with public procurement could become little more than a show, patient mobility could get lip-service but be made a bureaucratic nightmare for those who try it, or some form of OMC might deter the Court from extending competencies altogether. Almost any policy, perhaps especially EU policy, can be made a nonsense.

Second, there are limits to what the EU can do. Just as there is no obvious European social model, there is no obvious health system model on hand. The diversity of health care systems – the same diversity that makes a social model a chimera – makes it difficult for the EU to start to force systems to converge. It can inflict poorly understood compliance, transition and opportunity costs on health care systems, but it cannot create a model because of its tiny budget and the political and practical differences between systems.

Third, as the chapters in this book should have shown, there are also tremendous differences in the interaction between different member states, and their health systems, and the EU (see also Greer and Rauscher 2008; Martinsen and Vrangbaek 2008; Obermaier 2008a). The interpretation, litigation, implementation and effects of a given rule will vary between systems. Below a certain level of abstraction and EU law, no rule will help us; we cannot generalize between the UK and Spain because the health systems of the UK and the health systems of Spain differ in crucial details, as do their citizens, competition law authorities, regional governments and judges.

These might look like reasons to relax. They are not. They are actually reasons to engage. Whether European Union health policy is a boon, a disaster or simply an obscure Belgian sideshow depends on actions that are taken now. One of the most important facts about politics is that it is often easiest to exercise influence at the times when the fewest people are disposed to exercise influence. That is because an effective intervention at the first stages of thinking can create or kill policy ideas that would take on lives of their own. At later stages, somebody else – and possibly somebody less legitimate or qualified – has already taken decisions. Member states, and most health policy leaders, quite predictably (Conant 2002) tried ignoring the EU for years after *Kohll* and *Decker* (let alone older decisions such as *Grogan*). That did not work; by the time they began to engage politically with EU health policy, the Court had already worked out a little corpus of law and applied it to hospital and non-hospital care, social insurance systems and national health systems. It was, in *Watts*, closing in on a definition of an appropriate waiting time and an obligation to price all transactions within health services. Ignoring it had not evidently made it go away. And that was before there were as many EU actors and entrepreneurs looking for ways to develop EU health policies. DG Sanco was created in recognizable form only in 1997, after all; before that, the Commission did not have a specialized unit for intervention in health. Health lobbyists in Brussels were few and far between in 1998 and much less numerous than European federations interested in one aspect or another of health to whom lobbying the EU had never occurred.

This book has shown the development and outlines of the new EU health policy community. EU institutions' autonomous activity – above all decisions of the ECJ, but also the enterprising activities of the Commission – have created the health policies, and the politics of lobbies and member state engagement follow. There is essentially no democratic legitimacy to the procedure. 'Civil society' and the preferences of Europe's citizens are routinely invoked by advocates of EU policies, but neither the presence of Brussels health lobbyists (a reaction to EU institutions' activities) nor flawed readings of vague questions in *Eurobarometer* legitimize the extensive, intrusive, deregulatory policies we have seen (also Höpner and Schäfer 2008). What little democratic legitimacy there is to EU health policy comes from the small amount that the European Parliament and Council get to legislate, and those decisions are so framed by the activities of the Court and Commission as to add only slightly to the democratic credentials of EU health policymaking.

The interactions of the EU institutions, member state governments, lobbies and an unpredictable and ever-widening circle of stakeholders will also dictate the impact of current and future EU health policies. That will include effects not found in law textbooks but important in policy debate. It is only responsible for policymakers to consider worst-case scenarios and unintended consequences; a comforting legal opinion is only of so much use when the stakes are so high and the law as thin as it is in competition law or public procurement. Even if the consequences are disastrous, the EU institutions will not bear them; efficiency of the EU is precisely because it outsources policy and its costs onto member states.

Furthermore, the mere fact that EU law can have laudable aims does not exclude its having unintended consequences. Consider one example of a little-discussed issue that is developing now: corruption. Corruption has not entered the EU discussion at all, or is discussed, rightly, as something endemic in most Eastern European and Mediterranean systems. But European integration, however often justified by transparency, can produce the opposite and that is likely to be the case in health care (Warner 2007). The basic problem is that cross-border patient mobility encourages all sorts of patient regulatory arbitrage. Member state financial controls depend on particular kinds of information and do not travel well, or always make sense, in cross-border settings. This is, of course, a simple call for member states to somehow redesign their forms to prevent corruption – a cost to them. It is also a likely future justification for further European integration: perhaps work on information systems could improve the situation! Costs of corruption might be dwarfed by other issues, or by pre-existing corruption. But it is an example of unintended consequences of the EU policy. The EU policy process is relatively predictable in its regulatory bent and constant expansion of EU powers. The exact natures of the politics and the speed of expansion are, however, to be determined.

FUTURE EU HEALTH POLICY MODELS

At the present, that suggests a future for EU health policy: an intellectual model from northwest Europe, one that is carefully adapted in order to fit well with the French, German, UK and perhaps Belgian and Scandinavian health care systems. Given the silence of member states and lobbies alike from the Mediterranean and Eastern Europe, we can assume that it is there that we will be most likely to find systems paying large transition costs, policy experts complaining of Brussels impositions, scholars writing about 'misfit' between domestic institutions and EU policy, and complaints of bad implementation and denial of Europeans' citizenship rights.

What might such an outcome be? We can broadly distinguish 'minimal', 'medium' and 'maximal' scenarios (as in Hazell 1999). This stands regardless of the intellectual, legal and bureaucratic bases supporting policy (as in Chapter 3 and Greer 2008a). The exact nature of EU policies obviously interests EU policy experts, but need not interest everybody in health care who has to live with it. From the point of view of health care systems, public health leaders and policy advocates, rather than EU experts, what is the range of outcomes?

Minimal

The minimalist scenario delivers what is arguably the main objective of the Commission: incorporation of health care into a European polity. If the basic objective of European integration is to allow European citizens to be treated equally anywhere in the EU, then patient mobility and professional mobility are obviously important goals. But, as seen in the draft directive on professional mobility, this is compatible with a very short list of implementable policies (the directive's effectively impossible demands for quality reporting are a different kind of issue). So the minimal option would mean a great deal of what is called 'box-ticking' in the British Isles: 'transparent' announcements of contracts for services, wide swathes of public services exempt from competition, public procurement law, a largely theoretical commitment to patient mobility outside of social security law, and in general a grudging enforcement of market regulation.

There are tremendous pressures for such a minimalist form of EU health policy, from those who see the benefits of neither EU involvement nor its market-making activities. If the constraints that the EU places on health care services could be reduced, there might be more scope for a genuinely positive EU policy that would solve problems such as the wide disparities in cancer survival, a real problem that is by no means solved by arguments about public procurement. In this direction, Maurizio Ferrera outlines ways that solid legal protection for Services of General interest could block further activities by the Court, and could be coupled with new EU funds or uses of existing ones in support of convergent welfare standards (one idea might be a European foundation to purchase specialist care for rare diseases, an idea that would make a positive EU contribution without the Commission networking that came with its scheme for 'centres of reference') (Ferrera 2009).

So this mini model is imaginable, and many people in health policy would like to see it. Fundamentally, it would be an equilibrium in which health care systems pay lip-service to compliance with a wide range of EU law, including a polity-building goal of patient mobility that the Commission could advertise even if it runs into an Austrian snowbank when a German with a broken leg tries to claim his or her rights. But as an argument for complacency, it has two profound weaknesses. First, the EU is a powerful machine for expanding its own competencies. All those networks, meetings and declarations, such as the public campaign supporting the European Year of Workers' Mobility (2006, for those who missed it), are for a reason. Will the EU public health agenda influence public health advocates in many member states? The answer might be yes. Will *engrenage* in general create EU-wide networks of officials and experts who lobby for their substantive interest to be pursued at the EU level? It has in many other cases.

Second, nobody affiliated with the status quo should be cheered by the dictum that EU policies are only *really* implemented when there are domestic lobbies for their implementation. For a start, legitimate laws that are applied seriously are a good goal in a democracy. But beyond that, what is to say that no such lobby will emerge and take up the tools the Court provided? They have in other, unlikely areas (Conant 2002; Falkner et al. 2005; M. Smith 2005), and seemingly ignorable ECJ decisions have turned into powerful deregulating tools in the hands of lobbies and litigants.

Medium

A midi model would mean application of EU law, but with wide variation among member states. It takes off from two fundamental truths about the implementation of EU law. First, transposition (turning a directive into member state law) is not the same as legislation (passing a law, including or justified by the directive), which is not the same thing as implementation (having an effect, presumably the desired one). Professional mobility shows us the scope for member states to agree to mobility, agree that German nurses (who cannot insert intravenous needles) are equal to British nurses, and then operate the system in accordance with their own needs by upholding standards as much as they choose. So in areas where there is legislation, there can still be enormous variation between member states.

Second, as stated so often here, legislation is only a small part of what the EU does. On the one hand, hard law is implemented by member state courts and competition authorities interpreting EU law and member state law, so the exact meaning of competition or state aids law might vary from member state to member state. On the other, soft law depends on political will and policy communities that are highly variable. So the Open Method of Co-ordination in health, like OECD data, might look like a waste of paper in one member state and yet have been an important instrument in another. Again, this means that some member states would be prone to listen, and others not, and the result would be variability.

This scenario would be distinctive from the minimal scenario in that there would be areas, and member states, where the EU had serious effects. It would be distinctive from the maximal scenario in that reading EU documents would tell patients and providers next to nothing about their actual experience. It would be stable in so far as most EU regulatory policies tend to mean different things in the 27 member states. It would also benefit from the current difficulty of legislating in the EU, which requires so many cross-cutting majorities as to substantially narrow the scope of potential legislative change. But it would be unstable in so far as regulatory and quality arbitrage created pressures from litigants, lobbies, the Court or the Commission (or even outraged member states) for tighter EU law and as a range of policies and networks started to surround the Commission with lobbies demanding an EU action for their topic of interest.

Maximal

Finally, the maximal scenario would apply many of the basic dicta of EU market and political integration. There would be patient mobility, public procurement, state aids, competition, professional mobility and a host of other legal regimes. Health interest groups would understand that they had to incorporate Brussels into their political strategies no matter the issue, and that going to Brussels might be the most effective way to pursue their goals.

First and foremost, it would be deregulating, reregulating and more or less privatizing. New regulation could be onerous, but would be in the interests of promoting competition. The effect of holding public and private providers to the same standard, clamping down on subsidies to public operators, putting more reliance on contract-ing and competitive tendering for services, and implementing internal market law (under the guise of patient and professional mobility) would create both pressures to create markets and opportunities to do it as part of the required reforms. It would empower those who create markets and speed the development of new businesses com-peting for health care contracts. In short, it would turn the health systems of Europe into more of a market: not a stretch, given the documented ability of EU institutional entrepreneurs to turn a nat-ural monopoly like electricity into an object of liberalization (Jabko 2006).

There would be quality arbitrage; if the demands for presentation of quality indicators were somehow to be answered, it is not hard to imagine better-off patients starting to use their mobility more ser-iously. There would be regulatory arbitrage, with providers taking advantage of stronger or weaker regulatory systems as made sense for their marketing: for example, operating competitive, patient-facing facilities in states with good reputations and farming laboratory work out to cheaper member states. There would be cost arbitrage. There would also probably be corruption. The overall result would be the development of markets in health care, probably with a strong bias towards serving patients with the skills and self-esteem to use foreign providers and the wealth to attract new entrants.

The key attributes of this scenario are that it would mean that the EU was a major force shaping health policy by demanding rough compliance with a variety of laws designed to promote competition and non-discrimination; that it would be serious about promoting patient mobility; and that health care providers would in general be subject to much of EU internal market law. A combination of public finance and competitive private provision would be a likely intel-lectual model.

This is something of a nightmare scenario for many member states and health stakeholders, who would see it as both an insult to dem-ocracy and a massive blow to the solidarity and egalitarianism of health systems. The likeliest way to create it would be to leave the development of EU health policy in the hands of the ECJ and the Commission. Opponents of the Constitution and Lisbon treaties, by leaving the EU with a set of rules that make legislation very difficult, supported this outcome. The golden age of ECJ power was the 1970s and early 1980s, when member states agreed to seek unanimity in policy. Under current rules, legislating is very difficult, so we might be about to see a new golden age for the Court. Given what it has done to EU health law in its years on the defensive, this might cause some worry.

DOING SOMETHING ABOUT IT

Who will decide what happens? The Commission and Court created the health policy agenda, but they no longer control it in its entirety. Engaging now is still effective; the range of options in EU health policy is narrowing, but only slowly, and there is still a considerable level of uncertainty for those who engage. Who is most likely to engage at early stages? Advocates will engage at the speed that their member organizations are prone to engage in lobbying, meaning that stakeholders with more money, and from northwestern Europe, will move fastest in most cases, and Mediterranean or Eastern countries will lag. We must hope that their states and regional governments effectively represent them, but this is an unlikely notion, if Spain is anything to go by and the secondary literature otherwise is accurate. But there is still a major element of chance. At the origin of many EU health lobbies, especially in health care, is a single individual or a couple of entrepreneurs. That is why most EU health lobbyists spend so much time lobbying backward to persuade their members or home offices that they are a good use of resources. There might come a time when every serious health organization is somehow tied into EU interest representation, but currently entrepreneurship, chance and different countries' propensities to lobby all matter.

Member states are not far ahead of stakeholders. One official from a competent member state put it to me in 2006 that every member state 'has put at least one good person on it', and named a few. Since then, I have asked other member state officials if they agree. Most comment on that interviewee's optimism. What really explains member state engagement, as the preceding chapters should have made clear, is member state politics. And that throws us into a set of unpleasant conclusions: not only are there deep structural reasons why some countries have more coherent and thought-out positions than others, but also those problematic structures are often the solutions' even greater problems. It would be a stretch to argue that we should rewrite a constitution to enhance EU representation.

If EU health policy continues to grow in importance, eventually every EU member state will have a reasonably competent EU health policy apparatus at the diplomatic and departmental level, a European culture in at least a few parts of the health ministries, and some in-house knowledge of the issues and networks required to influence and implement EU policies. But by then the policy issues are likely to be much smaller and the outlines of policy set. Even in the glacial EU, a critical juncture does not last forever, and once it is over the costs of moving to a different trajectory can be very high.

Much Europeanization literature comments on this phenomenon (Börzel 2007): some member states 'upload' their model to EU policy, thereby influencing EU policies in ways that ease their transition (and spread the benefits of their model) but create transition and adaptation problems for other member states. Quite often, the fluency with which a member state and its lobbies advocate for the model, early in the deliberative level of policy, determines which models get uploaded. Perhaps a member state has a good model that EU health policy might imitate, or respect. If it is not active on the deliberative and departmental level now, its future will be one of rearguard actions to reduce the costs of EU health policy rather than presentations of the virtues of its approach.

CONCLUSION: FEEDBACKS

Meanwhile, policymakers should be attentive to the secondary effects of EU health policy development. So far we have seen the direct effects: the policy responses such as amendment of German social law or UK legislation to incorporate patient mobility, and the political responses as a shifting constellation of member states, advocates, and DGs try to formulate the political arena.

The next step is to see what effects EU health policy has on EU health systems, and then, further, what effects that has on the politics of EU health policymaking. This is another layer of strategic, future-oriented analysis. It is where political analysts must start to turn their attention. Right now the politics of EU health policy are almost out of a textbook on European integration, with initiatives led by the Court and then the Commission being met by a developing constellation of lobbyists and member states applying their own models. But the actors themselves will be changed by their experience of EU health law. They will not change much, or grow much more, under a minimal scenario, but if EU health policy continues to develop it will start to affect real EU health systems and the political actors within. Part of the challenge will be understanding its effects on German dentists who contract with Hungarian laboratories, or British retirees using Spanish care without going through the right social security law, or the effects on French autonomy of a possibly required OMC in health written into the Lisbon treaty. But the next step will be to trace the interventions of German dentists in EU policymaking in Brussels or Berlin, or the effects on the British charity Age Concern of its new offices and concerns in Spain, or the effects on Spanish governments of their new responsibilities to elderly Londoners, or the results of French efforts to turn the OMC to ends its political leaders seek.

The existence of EU health policy is undeniable. The secret garden is being turned into a public park. Its turbulence is also undeniable; the chaos of different policy models and uncertainty about the eventual impact of regulations on health politics, systems and patients is characteristic of a policy field in formation. That chaos is the most promising time to act. Doing something about it is the challenge right now for those who would promote the autonomy of health policy and the importance of health right now. But the next intellectual challenge is coming. Not only must the former inhabitants of the secret garden adapt to its new openness; they must also understand how they will interact in the future, outside its protective, or constraining, walls.

REFERENCES

Ackers, L. and P. Dwyer (2002) *Senior Citizenship? Retirement, Migration and Welfare in the European Union*, Policy, Bristol.

Aja, E. (1999) *El Estado Autónomico: Federalismo y Hechos Diferenciales*, Alianza, Madrid.

Alber, J. (2006) The European Social Model and the United States, *European Union Politics* 7, 393–419.

Alford, R. (1975) *Health Care Politics: Ideological and Interest Group Barriers to Reform*, University of Chicago Press, Chicago, IL.

Altenstetter, C. (2005) Bridging European and member state implementation: The case of medical goods, in vitro diagnostics and equipment, in: M. Steffen (ed.) *Health Governance in Europe: Issues, Challenges and Theories*, Routledge, New York, 81–112.

Alter, K. J. (1998) Who are the 'Masters of the Treaty'? European governments and the European Court of Justice, *International Organization* 52, 121–147.

Anderson, J. J. (1997) Hard interests, soft power, and Germany's changing role in Europe, in: P. Katzenstein (ed.) *Tamed Power: Germany in Europe*, Cornell University Press, Ithaca, NY, 49–79.

Baisnée, O. (2005) The French press and the European Union: The challenge of Community news, in: H. Drake (ed.) *French Relations with the European Union*, Routledge, Abingdon, 124–145.

Balfour, S. and A. Quiroga (2007) *The Reinvention of Spain: Nation and Identity since Democracy*, Oxford University Press, Oxford.

Balme, R. and C. Woll (2005) France: Between integration and national sovereignty, in: S. Bulmer and C. Lequesne (eds) *The Member States of the European Union*, Oxford University Press, Oxford, 97–118.

Bandelow, N. C. (2007) Ärtzeverbände: Niedergang eines Erfolgsmodells?, in: T. von Winter and U. Willems (eds) *Interessenverbände in Deutschland*, VS Verlag für Sozialwissenschaften, Wiesbaden, 271–293.

Barroso, J. M. (2005) Working together for growth and jobs: A new start for the Lisbon Strategy, Remarks to the Conference of Presidents, European Parliament, Brussels.

Bartolini, S. (2005) *Restructuring Europe: Centre Formation, System Building and Political Structuring between the Nation-State and the European Union*, Oxford University Press, Oxford.

Bell, D. S. (2000) *Presidential Power in Fifth Republic France*, Berg, Oxford.

Beyers, J. (2002) Gaining and seeking access: The European adaptation of domestic interest associations, *European Journal of Political Research* 41, 585–612.

Beyers, J., R. Eising and W. Maloney (2009) Much we study, little we know? The study of interest group politics in Europe and elsewhere, *West European Politics* 31 (6), 1103–1128.

Bogdanor, V. (ed.) (2005) *Joined-up Government*, British Academy and Oxford University Press, Oxford.

Bomberg, E. and A. C.-G. Stubb (eds) (2003) *The European Union: How Does It Work?*, Oxford University Press, Oxford.

Borras, S. and K. Jacobsson (2004) The open method of co-ordination and new governance patterns in the EU, *Journal of European Public Policy* 11, 185–208.

Börzel, T. (2007) Environmental policy, in: P. Graziano and M. P. Vink (eds) *Europeanization: New Research Agendas*, Palgrave Macmillan, Basingstoke, 226–238.

Bridges, E. (1950) *Portrait of a Profession: The Civil Service Tradition*, Cambridge University Press, London.

Buck, T. and I. Bickerton (2005) Changes to services directive on the cards, *Financial Times* (London), 7, 17 April.

Bulmer, S. (1997) Shaping the rules? The constitutive politics of the European Union and German power, in: P. Katzenstein (ed.) *Tamed Power: Germany in Europe*, Cornell University Press, Ithaca, NY, 1–48.

Bulmer, S. and M. Burch (1998) Organizing for Europe: Whitehall, the British State, and European Union, *Public Administration* 76, 601–628.

Bulpitt, J. (1983) *Territory and Power in the United Kingdom: An Interpretation*, Manchester University Press, Manchester.

Bursens, P. (2007) State structures, in: P. Graziano and M. P. Vink (eds) *Europeanization: New Research Agendas*, Palgrave Macmillan, Basingstoke, 115–127.

Busse, R., M. Wismar and P. C. Berman (eds) (2002) *The European Union and Health Services: The Impact of the Single European Market on Member States*, IOS and European Health Management Association, Amsterdam.

Carmichael, P. (2002) The Northern Ireland Civil Service: Characteristics and trends since 1970, *Public Administration* 80, 23–49.

Castles, F. G. (2004) *The Future of the Welfare State: Crisis Myths and Crisis Realities*, Oxford University Press, Oxford.

Chevallier, J. (1997) L'Elite politico-administrative: Une interpénétration discutée, *Pouvoirs* 80, 89–100.

Chevallier, J. (2005) La Reconfiguration de l'administration centrale, *Revue française d'administration publique* 116, 715–726.

Cini, M. (ed.) (2003) *European Union Politics*, Oxford University Press, Oxford.

Clergeau, C. (2005) European food safety polices: Between a single market and a political crisis, in: M. Steffen (ed.) *The Governance of Health in Europe*, Routledge, London, 113–133.

Clift, B. (2007) Europeanizing social models?, *Journal of European Integration* 29, 249–254.

Closa, C. (ed.) (2001) *La Europeización del sistema politico español*, ISTMO, Madrid.

Closa, C. and P. Heywood (2004) *Spain and the European Union*, Palgrave Macmillan, Basingstoke.

Coen, D. (ed.) (2007) *EU Lobbying: Empirical and Theoretical Studies*, Routledge, Abingdon.

Coen, D. and C. Dannreuther (2003) Differentiated Europeanization: Large and small firms in the EU policy process, in: K. Featherstone and C. Radaelli (eds) *The Politics of Europeanization*, Oxford University Press, Oxford, 255–277.

Coen, D. and J. Richardson (eds) (2009) *Lobbying the European Union: Institutions, Actors, and Issues*, Oxford University Press, Oxford.

Commissariat général du Plan (2002) *Organiser la politique européenne et internationale de la France, rapport du groupe de réflexion présidé par l'Amiral Jacques Lanxade, Nicolas Tenzer rapporteur général*, La Documentation française, Paris.

Commission of the European Communities (2000) *Social Policy Agenda COM(2000)379*, Commission of the European Communities, Brussels.

Conant, L. (2002) *Justice Contained: Law and Politics in the European Union*, Cornell University Press, Ithaca, NY.

Conferencia para asuntos relacionados con las Comunidades Europeas (2006) *'Guía de buenas prácticas' para la aplicación del acuedo sobre el sistema de representación autonómica en las formaciones del consejo de la Unión Europea*, Ministerio de Administraciones Públicas, Madrid.

Costa, O. and J.-P. Daloz (2005) How French policy-makers see themselves, in: H. Drake (ed.) *French Relations with the European Union*, Routledge, Abingdon, 21–41.

Cour des Comptes (2004) L'Evolution du rôle de la direction générale de la santé, in: C. d. Comptes (ed.) *Rapport annuel*, Cour des Comptes, Paris, 141–170.

Cram, L. (1993) Calling the tune without paying the piper? Social policy regulation: The role of the Commission in European Community Social Policy, *Policy and Politics* 21, 135–146.

Cram, L. (1997) *Policy-Making in the European Union: Conceptual Lenses and the Integration Process*, Routledge, London.

Dawson, S. and Z. Morris (2008) Introduction, in: S. Dawson and Z. Morris (eds) *Future Public Health: Burdens, Challenges and Opportunities*, Palgrave Macmillan, Basingstoke, 1–12.

Dawson, D. and L. Mountford (2008) *Health Care Services and the Single European Market*, Office of Health Economics, London.

Dehousse, R. (ed.) (2004) *L'Europe sans Bruxelles? Une analyse de la methode ouverte de co-ordination*, L'Harmattan, Paris.

Dehousse, R., F. Deloche-Gaudez and O. Duhamel (2006) *Elargissement: Comment l'Europe s'adapte*, Presses de Sciences Po, Paris.

Díez Medrano, J. (2000) *Framing Europe: Attitudes to European Integration in Germany, Spain, and the United Kingdom*, Princeton University Press, Princeton, NJ.

Drake, H. (ed.) (2005) *French Relations with the European Union*, Routledge, Abingdon.

Dutton, P. V. (2007) *Differential Diagnoses: A Comparative History of Health Care Problems and Solutions in the United States and France*, Cornell University Press, Ithaca, NY.

Dyson, K. (2003) The Europeanization of German governance, in: S. Padgett, W. E. Paterson and G. Smith (eds) *Developments in German Politics 3*, Palgrave Macmillan, Basingstoke, 161–183.

Dyson, K. and K. H. Goetz (2003) Living with Europe: Power, constraint and contestation, in: K. Dyson and K. H. Goetz (eds)

Germany, Europe and the Politics of Constraint, Oxford University Press, Oxford, 3–35.

Egeberg, M. (2006) Europe's executive branch of government in the melting pot: An overview, in: M. Egeberg (ed.) *Multilevel Union Administration: The Transformation of Executive Politics in Europe*, Palgrave Macmillan, Basingstoke, 1–16.

Ehrel, C., L. Mandin and B. Palier (2005) The leverage effect: The open method of co-ordination in France, in: J. Zeitlin and P. Pochet (eds) *The Open Method of Coordination in Action: The European Employment and Social Inclusion Strategies*, PIE and Peter Lang, Brussels, 217–248.

Epp, C. R. (1998) *The Rights Revolution: Lawyers, Activists, and Supreme Courts – A Comparative Perspective*, University of Chicago Press, Chicago, IL.

Esping-Andersen, G. (1990) *The Three Worlds of Welfare Capitalism*, Princeton University Press, Princeton, NJ.

Ettelt, S., N. Mays, K. Chevrul, A. Nikolentzos, S. Thomson and E. Nolte (2008) *How Responsible are Ministries of Health for Deciding What Should be Collectively Funded in Health Systems?*, European Health Policy Group (LSE), London.

Eurobarometer (2008) *Eurobarometer 69: Public Opinion in the European Union, Spring 2008*, DG Communication, Brussels.

Eymeri, J.-M. (2001) *La Fabrique des énarques*, Economica, Paris.

Eymeri, J.-M. (2002) Définir 'la position de la France' dans l'Union européenne: La médiation inerministérielle des généralistes du SCGI, in: O. Nay and A. Smith (eds) *Le Gouvernement du compromis: Courtiers et généralistes dans l'action politique*, Economica, Paris, 140–175.

Faber, J.-C. (2004) The European Blood Directive: A new era of blood regulation has begun, *Transfusion Medicine* 14, 257–273.

Fairbrass, J. (2003) The Europeanization of business interest representation: UK and French firms compared, *Comparative European Politics* 1, 313–334.

Falkner, G., M. Hartlapp and O. Treib (2007) Worlds of compliance: Why leading approaches to European Union implementation are only 'sometimes-true' theories, *European Journal of Political Research* 46, 395–416.

Falkner, G., O. Treib, M. Hartlapp and S. Leiber (2005) *Complying with Europe: EU Harmonisation and Soft Law in the Member States*, Cambridge University Press, Cambridge.

Farrell, A.-M. (2005) The emergence of EU governance in public health: The case of blood policy and regulation, in: M. Steffen (ed.) *Health Governance in Europe*, Routledge, London, 134–151.

Farrell, D. M. and R. Scully (2007) *Representing Europe's Citizens?*, Oxford University Press, Oxford.

Fernández Farreres, G. (ed.) (2006) *El Régimen Jurídico de las Subvenciones: Derecho Español y Communitario*, Consejo General del Poder Judicial, Madrid.

Ferrara, M. (1996) The 'Southern Model' of welfare in social Europe, *Journal of European Social Policy* 6, 17–37.

Ferrera, M. (2005) *The Boundaries of Welfare: European Integration and the New Spatial Politics of Social Protection*, Oxford University Press, Oxford.

Ferrera, M. (2009) National welfare states and European integration: Dilemmas and perspectives, *Journal of Common Market Studies*.

Fligstein, N. (2008) *Euroclash: The EU, European Identity, and the Future of Europe*, Oxford University Press, Oxford.

Fouilleux, E., J. de Maillard and A. Smith (2004) Les Groupes de Travail du Conseil: Nerf de la production des politiques européennes?, in: C. Lequesne and Y. Surel (eds) *L'Intégration européenne*, Presses de Sciences Po, Paris, 143–184.

Franc, C. and D. Polton (2004) New governance arrangements for French health insurance, *Eurohealth* 12, 27–29.

Fundación de Ciencias de la Salud (ed.) (1997) *La Dimension Europea de la Política Sanitaria Nacional y Regional*, Doce Calles, Aranjuez.

Gallego, R. (2003) Public management policymaking in Spain 1982–1996: Policy entrepreneurship and (in)opportunity windows, *International Public Management Journal* 6, 283–307.

Gallego, R., R. Gomà and J. Subirats (2002) *Els Règims Autonòmics de Benestar*, Instit d'Estudis Autonòmics, Barcelona.

Gallego, R., R. Gomà and J. Subirats (2003) *Estado de bienestar i Comunidades Autónomas*, Tecnos, Madrid.

Genieys, W. and M. Smyrl (2008) Inside the Autonomous State: Programmatic elites in the reform of French health policy, *Governance* 21, 75–93.

Geuijen, K., P. 't Hart and K. Yesilkagit (2007) Dutch Eurocrats at work: Getting things done in Europe, in: R. A. W. Rhodes, P. 't Hart and M. Noordegraf (eds) *Observing Government Elites: Up Close and Personal*, Palgrave Macmillan, Basingstoke, 131–159.

Giddens, A., P. Diamond and R. Liddle (2006) *Global Europe, Social Europe*, Polity, Cambridge.

Gobrecht, J. (1999) National reactions to Kohll and Decker, *Euro-health* 5, 16–17.

Goetschy, J. (2006) Taking stock of social Europe: Is there such a thing as a Community Social Model?', in: M. Jepsen and A. Serrano Pascual (eds) *Unwrapping the European Social Model*, Policy, Bristol.

Goetz, K. (2007) German officials and the federal policy process: The decline of sectional leadership, in: E. C. Page and V. Wright (eds) *From the Active to the Enabling State: The Changing Role of Top Officials in European Nations*, Palgrave, Basingstoke, 164–188.

Goldsmith, M. (2003) Variable geometry, multilevel governance: European integration and subnational government in the new millennium, in: K. Featherstone and C. Radaelli (eds) *The Politics of Europeanization*, Oxford University Press, Oxford, 112–133.

Goodhart, D. (1998) Social dumping within the EU, in: D. Hine and H. Kassim (eds) *Beyond the Market: The EU and National Social Policy*, Routledge, London.

Greenwood, J. (2002) Advocacy, influence and persuasion: Has it all been overdone?, in: A. Warleigh and J. Fairbrass (eds) *Influence and Interests in the European Union: The New Politics of Persuasion and Advocacy*, Europa, London 19–34.

Greenwood, J. (2003) *Interest Representation in the European Union*, Palgrave Macmillan, Basingstoke.

Greer, S. L. (2004) *Territorial Politics and Health Policy: UK Health Policy in Comparative Perspective*, Manchester University Press, Manchester.

Greer, S. L. (2005) Why do good politics make bad health policy?, in: C. Sausman and S. Dawson (eds) *Future Health Organisations and Systems*, Palgrave, Basingstoke, 105–128.

Greer, S. L. (2006a) *Responding to Europe: Government, NHS and Stakeholder Responses to the EU Health Challenge*, Nuffield Trust, London.

Greer, S. L. (2006b) Uninvited Europeanization: Neofunctionalism and the EU in health policy, *Journal of European Public Policy* 13, 134–152.

Greer, S. L. (2006c) A very English institution: Central and local in the English NHS, in: R. Hazell (ed.) *The English Question*, Manchester University Press, Manchester 194–219.

Greer, S. L. (2007a) The fragile divergence machine: Citizenship, policy divergence, and intergovernmental relations, in: A. Trench (ed.) *Devolution and Power in the United Kingdom*, Manchester University Press, Manchester, 136–159.

Greer, S. L. (2007b) *Nationalism and Self-Government: The Politics of Autonomy in Scotland and Catalonia*, State University of New York Press, Albany, NY.

Greer, S. L. (2008a) Choosing paths in European Union health policy: A political analysis of a critical juncture, *Journal of European Social Policy* 18, 219–231.

Greer, S. L. (2008b) The end of Whitehall?, in: R. Hazell (ed.) *Constitutional Futures Revisited*, Palgrave Macmillan, Basingstoke.

Greer, S. L. (2008c) *Power Struggle: The European Union and Health Care Services*, Observatoire Social Européen, Brussels.

Greer, S. L. (2009a) The changing world of European health lobbies, in: D. Coen and J. J. Richardson (eds) *Lobbying in the European Union*, Oxford University Press, Oxford.

Greer, S. L. (2009b) Ever closer union: Devolution, the European Union, and social citizenship rights, in: S. L. Greer (ed.) *Devolution and Social Citizenship Rights in the United Kingdom*, Policy, Bristol, 123–138.

Greer, S. L. (2009c) Options and the lack of options: Health care politics and policy, *Political Quarterly*.

Greer, S. L. and H. Jarman (2007a) *The Department of Health and the Civil Service: From Whitehall to Department of Delivery to Where?*, Nuffield Trust, London.

Greer, S. L. and H. Jarman (2007b) *What Whitehall?*, American Political Science Association, Chicago, IL.

Greer, S. L. and M. Mätzke (2009) Introduction, in: S. L. Greer (ed.) *Devolution and Social Citizenship in the United Kingdom*, Policy Press, Bristol.

Greer, S. L. and S. Rauscher (2008) When does market-marking make markets? EU health services policy at work – policy in the UK and Germany, Fourth Pan-European Conference of the ECPR Standing Group on European Union Politics, Riga.

Greer, S. L. and A. Trench (2008) *Health and Intergovernmental Relations in the Devolved United Kingdom*, Nuffield Trust, London.

Greer, S. L. and B. Vanhercke (2009) The hard politics of soft law, in: E. Mossialos, G. Permanand, R. Baeten and T. Hervey (eds) *Health Systems Governance in Europe: The Role of EU Law and Policy*, Cambridge University Press, Cambridge.

Greer, S. L., E. M. da Fonseca and C. Adolph (2008) Mobilizing bias in Europe: Lobbies, democracy, and EU health policy making, *European Union Politics* 9, 403–433.

Grossman, E. (ed.) (2005) *Lobbying et vie politique*, La Documentation française, Paris.

Grossman, E. and N. Sauger (2008) Political institutions under stress? Assessing the impact of European integration on French political institutions, in: E. Grossman (ed.) *France and the European Union: After the Referendum on the European Constitution*, Routledge, New York, 126–143.

Grossman, E. and S. Saurugger (2004) Challenging French interest groups: The State, Europe, and the international political system, *French Politics* 2 203–220.

Gunlicks, A. (2003) *The Länder and German Federalism*, Manchester University Press, Manchester.

Haas, E. B. (1958[2004]) *The Uniting of Europe: Political, Social, and Economic Forces 1950–1957*, University of Notre Dame Press, Notre Dame, IN.

Hacker, J. S. (2004) Reform without change, change without reform: The politics of U.S. health policy reform in cross-national perspective, in: M. A. Levin and M. Shapiro (eds) *Transatlantic Policy-making in an Age of Austerity: Diversity and Drift*, Georgetown University Press, Washington, DC, 13–63.

Haller, M. (2008) *European Integration as an Elite Process: The Failure of a Dream?*, Routledge, New York.

Ham, C. (2004) *Health Policy in Britain*, Palgrave Macmillan, Basingstoke.

Hancher, L. (2009) The EU pharmaceuticals market: Parameters and pathways, in: E. Mossialos, G. Permanand, R. Baeten and T. Hervey (eds) *Health Systems Governance in Europe: The Role of EU Law and Policy*, Cambridge University Press, Cambridge.

Hansen, S. B. (2006) *Globalization and the Politics of Pay*, Georgetown University Press, Washington, DC.

Harant, P. (2006) Hospital cooperation across French borders, in: M. Rosenmöller, M. McKee and R. Baeten (eds) *Patient Mobility in the European Union: Learning from Experience*, European Observatory on Health Systems and Policies, Brussels, 157–177.

Hassenteufel, P. and S. Hennion-Moreau (eds) (2003) *Concurrence et protection sociale en Europe*, Presses Universitaires de Rennes, Rennes.

Hassenteufel, P. and B. Palier (2005) Les Trompe-l'œil de la 'gouvernance' de l'assurance maladie: Contrastes franco-allemands, *Revue française d'administration publique* 113, 13–27.

Hatzopoulos, V. G. (2005) Health law and policy: The impact of the EU, in: G. De Búrca (ed.) *EU Law and the Welfare State*, Oxford University Press, Oxford, 111–168.

Hatzopoulos, V. (2009) Public procurement and state aid in national health care systems, in: E. Mossialos, G. Permanand, R. Baeten and T. Hervey (eds) *Health Systems Governance in Europe: The Role of EU Law and Policy*, Cambridge University Press, Cambridge.

Hauray, B. (2006) *L'Europe du médicament: Politique – Expertise – Intérêts privés*, Presses de Sciences Po, Paris.

Hayward, J. and V. Wright (2002) *Governing from the Centre: Core Executive Co-ordination in France*, Oxford University Press, Oxford.

Hazell, R. (ed.) (1999) *Constitutional Futures: A History of the Next Ten Years*, Oxford University Press, Oxford.

Hazell, R. and R. Rawlings (eds) (2005) *Devolution, Law Making and the Constitution*, Imprint Academic, Exeter.

Heclo, H. and A. Wildavsky (1974) *The Private Government of Public Money: Community and Policy inside British Politics*, University of California Press, Berkeley, CA.

Heisenberg, D. (2007) Informal decision-making in the Council: The secret of the EU's success?, in: S. Meunier and K. McNamara (eds) *Making History: European Integration and Institutional Change at Fifty*, Oxford University Press, Oxford, 67–88.

Hervey, T. and B. Vanhercke (2009) Health care and the EU: The law and policy patchwork, in: E. Mossialos, G. Permanand, R. Baeten and T. Hervey (eds) *Health Systems Governance in Europe: The Role of EU Law and Policy*, Cambridge University Press, Cambridge.

Hervey, T. K. and J. V. McHale (2004) *Health Law and the European Union*, Cambridge University Press, Cambridge.

Hix, S. (2005) *The Political System of the European Union*, Palgrave Macmillan, New York.

Hix, S., A. Noury and G. Roland (2007) *Democratic Politics in the European Parliament*, Cambridge University Press, Cambridge.

Höpner, M. and A. Schäfer (2008) Eine neue Phase der europäischen Integration: Legitimitätsdefizite europäischer Liberalisierungspolitik, in: M. Höpner and A. Schäfer (eds) *Die Politische Ökonomie der europäischen Integration*, Campus, Frankfurt, 129–257.

Holzinger, K. and C. Knill (2005) Cases and conditions of cross-national policy convergence, *Journal of European Public Policy* 12, 775–796.

Hooghe, L. and G. Marks (2001) *Multi-level Governance and European Integration*, Rowman & Littlefield, Lanham, MD.

Inspection générale des affaires sociales (2006a) *L'Utilisation des compétences médicales permettant à l'Etat d'assurer ses responsa-bilités dans le domaine de la santé au niveau local: Les médecins inspecteurs de santé publique*, La Documentation française, Paris.

Inspection générale des affaires sociales (2006b) *Rapport annuel; 2006: La dimension européenne des politiques sociales*, La Documentation française, Paris.

Iversen, T. and A. Wren (1998) Equality, employment, and budgetary restraint: The trilemma of the service economy, *World Politics* 50, 507–546.

Jabko, N. (2006) *Playing the Market: A Political Strategy for Uniting Europe 1985–2005*, Cornell University Press, Ithaca, NY.

Jeffery, C. (2005) Regions and the European Union: Letting them in, and leaving them alone, in: S. Weatherill (ed.) *The Role of Regions and Sub-National Actors in Europe*, Hart, Oxford, 33–46.

Jeffery, C. and R. Palmer (2007) The European Union, devolution, and power, in: A. Trench (ed.) *Devolution and Power in the United Kingdom*, Manchester University Press, Manchester, 218–238.

Jeffery, C. and W. E. Paterson (2004) Germany and European integration: A shifting of tectonic plates, in: H. Kitschelt and W. Streeck (eds) *Germany: Beyond the Stable State*, Frank Cass, London, 59–78.

Jepsen, M. and A. Serrano Pascual (2006) The concept of the ESM and supranational legitimacy-building, in: M. Jepsen and A. Serrano Pascual (eds) *Unwrapping the European Social Model*, Policy, Bristol.

Joana, J. and A. Smith (2002) *Les Commissaires européens: Technocrates, diplomates ou politiques?*, Presses de Sciences Po, Paris.

Joignot, F. (2008) *Gauche: Des idées pour une refondation*, Le Monde, Paris, 22 August.

Jordan, A. (2002) *The Europeanization of British Environmental Policy*, Palgrave, Basingstoke.

Jordan, A. (2003) The Europeanization of national government and policy: A departmental perspective, *British Journal of Political Science* 33, 261–282.

Jordan, A. and D. Liefferink (2004) Europeanization and convergence: Comparative conclusions, in: A. Jordan and D. Liefferink (eds) *Environmental Policy in Europe: The Europeanization of National Environmental Policy*, Routledge, New York, 224–246.

Jordan, A. and A. Schout (2006) *The Coordination of the European Union: Exploring the Capacities of Networked Governance*, Oxford University Press, Oxford.

Jupille, J. (2004) *Procedural Politics: Issues, Influence and Institutional Choice in the European Union*, Cambridge University Press, Cambridge.

Kamen, H. (2007) *The Disinherited: Exile and the Making of Spanish Culture, 1492–1975*, Harper, New York.

Kassim, H. (2008) France and the European Union under the Chirac presidency, in: A. Cole, P. Le Galès and J. Levy (eds) *Developments in French Politics 4*, Palgrave Macmillan, Basingstoke, 258–276.

Kassim, H., B. G. Peters and V. Wright (eds) (2000) *The National Co-ordination of EU Policy*, Oxford University Press, Oxford.

Kassim, H., A. Menon, B. G. Peters and V. Wright (eds) (2001) *The National Co-ordination of EU Policy: The European Level*, Oxford University Press, Oxford.

Katzenstein, P. (1987) *Policy and Politics in West Germany: The Growth of a Semisovereign State*, Temple University Press, Philadelphia, PA.

Keeler, J. and P. A. Hall (2001) Interest representation and the politics of protest, in: A. Guyomarch, P. A. Hall, J. Hayward and H. Machin (eds) *Developments in French Politics 2*, Palgrave Macmillan, Basingstoke, 50–67.

King, R., T. Warnes and A. Williams (2000) *Sunset Lives: British Retirement Migration to the Mediterranean*, Berg, Oxford.

Kingdon, J. W. (1995) *Agendas, Alternatives, and Public Policies*, HarperCollins, New York.

Klein, R. (2006) *The New Politics of the NHS: From Creation to Reinvention*, Radcliffe Medical, Oxford.

Kleinman, M. (2002) *A European Welfare State? European Union Social Policy in Context*, Palgrave Macmillan, Basingstoke.

Klenk, T. (2008) *Modernisierung der funktionalen Selbstverwaltung: Universitäten, Krankenkassen und andere Öffentliche Körperschaften*, Campus, Frankfurt.

Krasner, S. (1984) Approaches to the state: Alternative conceptions and historical dynamics, *Comparative Politics* 16, 223–246.

Laffan, B. (2007) Core executives, in: P. Graziano and M. P. Vink (eds) *Europeanization: New Research Agendas*, Palgrave Macmillan, Basingstoke, 128–140.

Lanceron, V. (2007) *Du SGCI au SGAE: Evolution d'une administration de coordination au coeur de la politique européenne de la France*, L'Harmattan, Paris.

Legido-Quigley, H., M. McKee, E. Nolte and I. A. Glinos (2008) *Assuring the Quality of Health Care in the European Union: A Case for Action*, Brussels: European Observatory on Health Care Systems and Policies.

Leibfried, S. and P. Pierson (1995) Semisovereign welfare states: Social policy in a multitiered Europe, in: S. Leibfried and P. Pierson (eds) *European Social Policy: Between Fragmentation and Integration*, Brookings Institution, Washington, DC, 43–77.

Lequesne, C. (1993) *Paris-Bruxelles: Comment se fait la politique européenne de la France*, Presses de Sciences Po, Paris.

Levy, J. and C. Skatch (2008) The return to a strong presidency, in: A. Cole, P. Le Galès and J. Levy (eds) *Developments in French Politics 4*, Palgrave Macmillan, Basingstoke, 198–215.

Liefferink, D. and A. Jordan (2004) Europeanization and policy convergence: A basis for comparative analysis, in: A. Jordan and D. Liefferink (eds) *Environmental Policy in Europe: The Europeanization of National Environmental Policy*, Routledge, New York, 15–31.

Lodge, G. and J. Mitchell (2006) Whitehall and the government of England, in: R. Hazell (ed.) *The English Question*, Manchester University Press, Manchester, 96–118.

Lodge, G. and B. Rogers (2006) *Whitehall's Black Box: Accountability and Performance in the Senior Civil Service*, Institute for Public Policy Research, London.

Loriaux, M. (1999) The French developmental state as myth and moral ambition, in: M. Woo-Cumings (ed.) *The Developmental State*, Cornell University Press, Ithaca, NY, 235–275.

McKee, M., E. Mossialos and R. Baeten (eds) (2002) *The Impact of EU Law on Health Care Systems*, Peter Lang, Brussels.

MacLennan, J. C. (2004) *España en Europa 1945–2000: Del ostracismo a la modernidad*, Marical Pons, Madrid.

Mahoney, C. (2008) *Brussels versus the Beltway: Advocacy in the United States and the European Union*, Georgetown University Press, Washington, DC.

Majone, G. (1994) The rise of the regulatory state in Europe, *West European Politics* 17, 77–102.

Majone, G. (1996) *Regulating Europe*, Routledge, London.

Mangenot, M. (2005) The Conseil d'Etat and Europe: Adapting the French administrative state, in: H. Drake (ed.) *French Relations with the European Union*, Routledge, Abingdon, 86–105.

Martinsen, D. S. and K. Vrangbaek (2008) The Europeanization of health care governance: Implementing the market imperatives of Europe, *Public Administration* 86, 169–184.

Mazey, S. and J. J. Richardson (eds) (1993) *Lobbying in the European Community*, Oxford University Press, Oxford.

Mazey, S. and J. J. Richardson (1995) Promiscuous policymaking: The European policy style?, in: C. Rhodes and S. Mazey (eds) *The State of the European Union: Building a European Polity?*, Lynne Rienner, Boulder, CO, 337–359.

Ménard, J. (2006) Le Directeur Général de la Santé, *Sève* 10, 33–42.

Mény, Y. (2001) National squares and European circle: The challenge of adjustment, in: A. Menon and V. Wright (eds) *From the Nation State to Europe? Essays in Honour of Jack Hayward*, Oxford University Press, Oxford.

Milner, S. (2005) Protection, reform and political will: France and the European Social Model, in: H. Drake (ed.) *French Relations with the European Union*, Routledge, Abingdon, 105–124.

Molina Álvarez de Cienfuegos, I. (2001) La adaptación a la Unión Europea del poder ejecutivo Español, in: C. Closa (ed.) *La Europeización del Sistema Político Español*, ISTMO, Madrid, 162–197.

Moran, M. (2003) *The British Regulatory State*, Oxford University Press, Oxford.

Morata, F. and G. Mateo (eds) (2007) *España en Europa, Europa en España*, CIDOB, Barcelona.

Morelle, A. (1996) *La Défaite de la santé publique*, Flammarion, Paris.

Mossialos, E. and M. McKee (eds) (2002) *EU Law and the Social Character of Health Care*, Peter Lang, Brussels.

Mossialos, E., M. Mrazek and T. Walley (eds) (2001) *Regulating Pharmaceuticals in Europe*, Open University Press, Maidenhead.

Mossialos, E., G. Permanand, R. Baeten and T. K. Hervey (eds) (2009) *Health Systems Governance in Europe: The Role of EU Law and Policy*, Cambridge University Press, Cambridge.

Newdick, C. (2009) The European Court of Justice, Trans-national health care and social citizenship: accidental death of a concept? *Wisconsin International Law Journal* 26 (3).

Oates, W. E. (1999) An essay on fiscal federalism, *Journal of Economic Literature* 37, 1120–1149.

Oberender, P. O., A. Hebborn and J. Zerth (2002) *Wachstumsmarkt Gesundheit*, Lucius and Lucius, Stuttgart.

Obermaier, A. J. (2008a) De-territorialization and de-structuring dynamics: The impact of ECJ patient mobility rulings on Germany, France, and the United Kingdom, Fourth Pan-European Conference of the ECPR Standing Group on EU Politics, Riga.

Obermaier, A. J. (2008b) Models of judicial politics revisited: The ECJ's judicial activism and self-restraint, Fourth Pan-European Conference of the ECPR Standing Group on the European Union, Riga.

Page, E. C. (1997) *People Who Run Europe*, Clarendon, Oxford.

Page, E. C. (2001) The European Union and the bureaucratic mode of production, in: A. Menon (ed.) *From the Nation State to Europe: Essays in Honour of Jack Hayward*, Oxford University Press, Oxford, 139–157.

Page, E. C. (2003) Europeanization and the persistence of national administrative systems, in: J. Hayward and A. Menon (eds) *Governing Europe*, Oxford University Press, Oxford, 162–178.

Page, E. C. (2005) Joined-up government and the civil service, in: V. Bogdanor (ed.) *Joined-Up Government*, Oxford University Press and British Academy, Oxford, 139–155.

Page, E. C. (2007) *Where Have All the Powers Gone? The UK Top Civil Service in Comparative Perspective*, American Political Science Association (www.apsanet.org), Chicago, IL.

Page, E. C. and B. Jenkins (2005) *Policy Bureaucracy: Government with a Cast of Thousands*, Oxford University Press, Oxford.

Page, E. C. and V. Wright (2007) Conclusions: The demystification of high bureaucratic office, in: E. C. Page and V. Wright (eds) *From the Active to the Enabling State: The Changing Role of Top Officials in European Nations*, Palgrave Macmillan, Basingstoke, 224–239.

Palier, B. (2005) *Gouverner la Sécurité Sociale*, Presses Universitaires de France, Paris.

Palier, B. and L. Petrescu (2007) France: Defending our model, in: J. Kvist and J. Saari (eds) *The Europeanisation of Social Protection*, Policy, Bristol, 61–76.

Parsons, C. (2003) *A Certain Idea of Europe*, Cornell University Press, Ithaca, NY.

Peeters, M., M. McKee and S. Merkur (2009) EU law and health professionals, in: E. Mossialos, G. Permanand, R. Baeten and T. Hervey (eds) *Health Systems Governance in Europe: The Role of EU Law and Policy*, Cambridge University Press, Cambridge.

Permanand, G. (2006) *EU Pharmaceutical Regulation: The Politics of Policy-Making*, Manchester University Press, Manchester.

Phelan, D. R. (1992) Right to life of the unborn v. promotion of trade in services: The European Court of Justice and the normative shaping of the European Union, *Modern Law Review* 55, 670–689.

Pierson, P. (2004) *Politics in Time: History, Institutions and Social Analysis*, Princeton University Press, Princeton, NJ.

Pierson, C. (2007) *Beyond the Welfare State? The New Political Economy of Welfare*, Polity, Oxford.

Pierson, P. and S. Leibfried (1995) The dynamics of social policy integration, in: S. Leibfried and P. Pierson (eds) *European Social Policy: Between Fragmentation and Integration*, Brookings Institution, Washington, DC, 423–465.

Poiares Maduro, M. (1998) *We the Court: The European Court of Justice and the European Economic Constitution*, Hart, Oxford.

Pounder, R. (2006) European junior doctors who work at night, *Eurohealth* 12, 5–7.

Prosser, T. (2005) *The Limits of Competition Law: Markets and Public Services*, Oxford University Press, Oxford.

Prosser, T. (2009) EU competition law and public services, in: E. Mossialos, G. Permanand, R. Baeten and T. Hervey (eds) *Health Systems Governance in Europe: The Role of EU Law and Policy*, Cambridge University Press, Cambridge.

Raunio, T. and S. Hix (2000) Backbenchers learn to fight back: European integration and parliamentary government, *West European Politics* 23, 142–168.

Rhodes, M. (1995) A regulatory conundrum: Industrial relations and the social dimension, in: S. Leibfried and P. Pierson (eds) *European Social Policy: Between Fragmentation and Integration*, Brookings Institution, Washington, DC, 78–128.

Richardson, J. (ed.) (2001) *European Union: Power and Policy-Making*, Routledge, London.

Rico Gómez, A., J. M. Freire and J. Gervás (2007) El sistema sanitario español (1976–2006): Factores de éxito en perspectiva internacional comparada, in: A. Espina (ed.) *Estado de Bienestar y competitividad: La experiencia europea*, Fundación Carolina y S. XXI Editores, Madrid, 401–444.

Risse, T. (2001) A European identity? Europeanization and the evolution of nation-state identities, in: M. Green Cowles, J. A. Caporaso and T. Risse (eds) *Transforming Europe: Europeanization and Domestic Change*, Cornell University Press, Ithaca, NY, 198–216.

Robert, C. (2007) L'Impossible 'modéle social européen', *Actes de la recherche en sciences sociales* 166–167, 94–109.

Rom, M. C. (2006) Policy races in the American states, in: K. Harrison (ed.) *Racing to the Bottom? Provincial Interdependence in the Canadian Federation*, University of British Columbia Press, Vancouver, BC.

Rosanvallon, P. (2004) *Le Modèle politique français: La société civil contre le jacobinisme de 1789 à nos jours*, Seuil, Paris.

Rose, R. (1987) *Ministers and Ministries: A Functional Analysis*, Clarendon, Oxford.

Rosenmöller, M. and M. Lluch (2006) Meeting the needs of long-term residents in Spain, in: M. Rosenmöller, M. McKee and R. Baeten (eds) *Patient Mobility in the European Union: Learning from Experience*, European Observatory on Health Systems and Policies, Brussels, 59–78.

Rouban, L. (1999) The senior civil service in France, in: E. C. Page and V. Wright (eds) *Bureaucratic Elites in Western European States*, Oxford University Press, Oxford, 65–89.

Rowland, D. (2006) *Mapping Communicable Disease Control Administration in the UK*, Nuffield Trust, London.

Rudzio, W. (2006) *Das politische System der Bundesrepublik Deutschland*, VS Verlag für Sozialwissenschaften, Wiesbaden.

Sairinen, R. and A. Lindholm (2004) Finland: A realistic pragmatist, in: A. Jordan and D. Liefferink (eds) *Environmental Policy in Europe: The Europeanization of National Environmental Policy*, Routledge, New York, 64–80.

Sauger, N. (2008) Attitudes towards Europe in France, in: A. Cole, P. Le Galès and J. Levy (eds) *Developments in French Politics 4*, Palgrave Macmillan, Basingstoke, 179–197.

Sauger, N., S. Brouard and E. Grossman (2007) *Les Français contre l'Europe? Les Sens du référendum du 29 mai 2005*, Presses de Sciences Po, Paris.

Sauron, J.-L. and V. Lanceron (2008) *L'Administration nationale et l'Europe: Acteurs nationaux et décisions communautaires*, La Documentation française, Paris.

Saurugger, S. and C. Woll (2008) Les Groupes d'intérêt, in: C. Belot, P. Magnette and S. Saurugger (eds) *Science politique de l'Union européenne*, Economica, Paris, 223–248.

Schäfer, A. and W. Streeck (2008) Korporatismus in der Europäischen Union, in: M. Höpner and A. Schäfer (eds) *Die Politische Ökonomie der europäischen Integration*, Campus, Frankfurt 203–240.

Scharpf, F. (1988) The joint decision trap: Lessons from German federalism and European integration, *Public Administration* 66, 238–278.

Scharpf, F. (1996) Negative and positive integration in the political economy of European welfare states, in: G. Marks, F. Scharpf, P. C. Schmitter and W. Streeck (eds) *Governance in the European Union*, Sage, London.

Scharpf, F., B. Reissert and F. Schnabel (1976) *Politikverflechtung:*

Theorie u. Empirie d. kooperativen Föderalismus in d. Bundesrepublik, Scriptor Verlag, Kronberg.

Schattschneider, E. E. (1960[1975]) *The Semisovereign People: A Realist's View of Democracy in America*, Dryden Press, Hinsdale, IL.

Schmidt, S. K. (2008) Europäische Integration zwischen judikativer und legislativer Politik, in: M. Höpner and A. Schäfer (eds) *Die Politische Ökonomie der europäischen Integration*, Campus, Frankfurt, 191–128.

Schmidt, V. A. (2006) *Democracy in Europe: The EU and National Polities*, Oxford University Press, Oxford.

Shore, C. (2000) *Building Europe: The Cultural Politics of European Integration*, Routledge, New York.

Shore, C. (2007) European integration in anthropological perspective: Studying the 'culture' of the EU civil service, in: R. A. W. Rhodes, P. 't Hart and M. Noordegraf (eds) *Observing Government Elites: Up Close and Personal*, Palgrave Macmillan, Basingstoke, 180–205.

Silio, F. (2001) Public procurement of goods and services: A legal analysis of the Spanish case, in: E. H. F. Gastein (ed.) *European Health Forum Gastein 2001*, EHFG, Bad Gastein, Austria, 121–141.

Simeon, R. (2006) Federalism and social justice: Thinking through the jungle, in: S. L. Greer (ed.) *Territory, Democracy, and Justice: Regionalism and Federalism in Western Democracies*, Palgrave Macmillan, Basingstoke.

Smith, A. (2006) The government of the European Union and a changing France, in: P. D. Culpepper, P. A. Hall and B. Palier (eds) *Changing France: The Politics that Markets Make*, Palgrave Macmillan, Basingstoke, 179–197.

Smith, M. P. (2005) *States of Liberalization: Redefining the Public Sector in Integrated Europe*, State University of New York Press, Albany, NY.

Solé-Tura, J. (1986) *Nacionalidades y Nacionalismos en España: Autonomías, Federalismo, Autodeterminación*, Alianza Editorial, Madrid.

Spence, D. (ed.) (2006) *The European Commission*, John Harper, London.

Steffen, M. (2000) The nation's blood: Medicine, justice, and the state in France, in: E. Feldman and R. Bayer (eds) *Blood Feuds: AIDS, Blood, and the Politics of Medical Disaster*, Oxford University Press, Oxford, 95–126.

Steffen, M. (ed.) (2005) *The Governance of Health in Europe*, Routledge, London.

Stein, H. (2003) On the road from Maastricht to a New Europe, *Eurohealth* 9, 17–21.

Stone Sweet, A. (2004) *The Judicial Construction of Europe*, Oxford University Press, Oxford.

Stone Sweet, A. (2005) Judicial authority and market integration in Europe, in: T. Ginsburg and R. A. Kagan (eds) *Institutions and Public Law: Comparative Approaches*, Peter Lang, Frankfurt, 99–140.

Streeck, W. (1996) Neo-voluntarism: A new European social policy regime?, in: G. Marks, F. Scharpf, P. C. Schmitter and W. Streeck (eds) *Governance in the European Union*, Sage, London.

Sturm, R. (2006) Die Länder in der deutschen und europäschen Mehrebenenpolitik, in: H. Schneider and H.-G. Wehling (eds) *Landespolitik in Deutschland*, VS Verlag für Sozialwissenschaften, Wiesbaden, 23–49.

Sturm, R. and H. Pehle (2006) *Das neue deutsche Regierungssystem: Die Europäisierung von Institutionen, Entscheidungs-prozessen und Politikfeldern in der Bundesrepublik Deutschland*, VS Verlag, Wiesbaden.

Subirats, J. (2006) The triumph and troubles of the Spanish model, in: S. L. Greer (ed.) *Territory, Justice, and Democracy*, Palgrave Macmillan, Basingstoke, 175–200.

Subirats, J. and R. Gallego (2002) *Veinte años de autonomías en España*, Alianza Editorial and CIS, Madrid.

Suhrcke, M., M. McKee, R. Sauto Arce, S. Tsolova and J. Mortensen (2005) *The Contribution of Health to the Economy in the European Union*, DG Health and Consumer Protection, Brussels.

Sundstreth, H. and L. F. Woods (2008) Cancer patients: partners for change, in: M. P. Coleman, D.-M. Alexe, T. Albreht and M. McKee (eds) *Responding to the Challenge of Cancer in Europe*, Institute of Public Health of the Republic of Slovenia, Ljubljana, 191–208.

Szukala, A. (2003) France: The European transformation of the French model, in: W. Wessels, A. Maurer and J. Mittag (eds) *Fifteen into One? The European Union and its Member States*, Manchester University Press, Manchester, 216–247.

Tarrow, S. (2004) Center–periphery alignments and political contention in late-modern Europe, in: C. K. Ansell and G. DiPalma (eds) *Restructuring Territoriality: Europe and the United States Compared*, Cambridge University Press, Cambridge, 45–65.

Thomson, S. and E. Mossialos (2007) Regulating private health insurance in the European Union: The implications of single market legislation and competition policy, *Journal of European Integration* 29, 89–107.

Thomson, S. and E. Mossialos (2009) Private health insurance and the internal market, in: E. Mossialos, G. Permanand, R. Baeten and T. Hervey (eds) *Health Systems Governance in Europe: The Role of EU Law and Policy*, Cambridge University Press, Cambridge.

Trench, A. (ed.) (2005) *The Dynamics of Devolution: The State of the Nations 2005*, Imprint Academic, Exeter.

Trench, A. (ed.) (2007) *Devolution and Power in the United Kingdom*, Manchester University Press, Manchester.

Trench, A. (ed.) (2008) *The State of the Nations 2008: Into the Third Term of Devolution in the UK*, Imprint Academic, Exeter.

Trubek, L., M. Nance and T. Hervey (2009) The construction of a healthier Europe: Lessons from the fight against cancer, *Wisconsin International Law Journal*.

Tsebelis, G. (2008) Thinking about the recent past and the future of the EU, *Journal of Common Market Studies* 46, 265–292.

Tsebelis, G. and S.-O. Prokosch (2007) The art of political manipulation in the European convention, *Journal of Common Market Studies* 45, 157–186.

Urgell, J. (ed.) (2003) *Donar protagonisme a Catalunya: Acció international i política de relacions exteriors catalana*, Pòrtic, Barcelona.

van Schendelen, R. (2002) *Machiavelli in Brussels: The Art of Lobbying the EU*, Amsterdam University Press, Amsterdam.

Wallace, H. (2005) Exercising power and influence in the European Union: The roles of member states, in: S. Bulmer and C. Lequesne (eds) *The Member States of the European Union*, Oxford University Press, Oxford, 25–44.

Warleigh, A. (2003) *Democracy in the European Union*, Sage, London.

Warner, C. M. (2007) *The Best System Money Can Buy: Corruption in the European Union*, Cornell University Press, Ithaca, NY.

Watts, R. L. (1999) *Comparing Federal Systems*, Institute of Intergovernmental Relations, Queens University, Kingston, Ontario.

Watts, R. L. (2006) Origins of cooperative and competitive federalism, in: S. L. Greer (ed.) *Territory, Democracy and Justice*, Palgrave Macmillan, Basingstoke.

Wessels, W., A. Maurer and J. Mittag (eds) (2003a) *Fifteen into One? The European Union and its Member States*, Manchester University Press, Manchester.

Wessels, W., A. Maurer and J. Mittag (2003b) Preface and major findings: The anatomy, the analysis, and the assessment of the 'beast', in: W. Wessels, A. Maurer and J. Mittag (eds) *Fifteen into One? The European Union and its Member States*, Manchester University Press, Manchester, xiii–xvii.

Westlake, M. and D. Galloway (eds) (2004) *The Council of the European Union*, John Harper, London.

Wincott, D. (2002) The Governance White Paper, the Commission and the search for legitimacy, in: A. Arnull and D. Wincott (eds) *Accountability and Legitimacy in the European Union*, Oxford University Press, Oxford, 379–398.

Wincott, D. (2003) Implementing the 'new open method of co-ordination' in the field of social inclusion, *Public Administration* 81, 533–553.

Wincott, D. (2004) Rights and Regulations in (the) Europe(an) Union): After national democracy?, in: L. Trägårdh (ed.) *After National Democracy: Rights, Law and Power in America and the New Europe*, Hart, Oxford, 79–102.

Woll, C. (2006) Lobbying in the European Union: From *sui generis* to a comparative perspective, *Journal of European Public Policy* 13, 456–469.

Woll, C. (2008) *Firm Interests: How Governments Shape Business Lobbying on Global Trade*, Cornell University Press, Ithaca, NY.

Wright, V. (1996) The national co-ordination of European policy-making: Negotiating the quagmire, in: J. J. Richardson (ed.) *European Union: Power and Policy-Making*, Routledge, London, 148–169.

Yach, D. (2005) Systems for health or healthcare systems?, in: S. Dawson and C. Sausman (eds) *Future Health Organisations and Systems*, Palgrave Macmillan, Basingstoke, 42–56.

Zimmerman, T. (2008) *Grenzüberschreitende Gesundheitsversorgung aus der Perspektive des deutschen Gesundheitswesens*, Nomos Verlagsgesellschaft, Baden-Baden.

INDEX